Healthy Together

Healthy Together

A Couple's Guide to Midlife Wellness

by Christine Langlois

A Canadian Living® Health Book

TELEMEDIA

McGraw-Hill Ryerson

Toronto Montréal New York Burr Ridge Bangkok Bogotá
Caracas Lisbon London Madrid Mexico City Milan
New Delhi Seoul Singapore Sydney Taipei

A Denise Schon/Kirsten Hanson Book
Copyright © 2000 Christine Langlois

**McGraw-Hill
Ryerson Limited**
A Subsidiary of The McGraw-Hill Companies

Published by McGraw-Hill Ryerson Limited
300 Water Street, Whitby, Ontario L I N 9B6
http://www.mcgrawhill.ca
Publisher: Joan Homewood

Canadian Cataloguing in Publication Data
Langlois, Christine (Christine Anne)
Healthy together: a couple's guide to midlife wellness
"A Canadian Living health book"
Includes index.
ISBN 0-07-086477-2
1. Couples – Health and hygiene. 2. Middle aged persons – Health and hygiene. I. Title
RA777.5.L36 2000   613' .0434   C00-930147X

Production: Denise Schon Books Inc.
Senior Researchers: Laurel Aziz, Susan Pedwell
Editor: Jennifer Glossop
Copy Editor: Jean Stinson
Researcher: Jaishree Drepaul
Index: Barbara Schon
Book Design: Counterpunch/Peter Ross
Front Cover Images (from left to right): Stone/Timothy Shonnard;
Stone/Martin Barraud; Stone/Dan Bosler

1 2 3 4 5 6 7 8 9 0 TRI 0 9 8 7 6 5 4 3 2 1 0

Printed and bound in Canada

for Christopher

Acknowledgments

EXPERT ADVISORS

The College of Family Physicians of Canada
Marshall Godwin   MD, CCFP, FCFP
Sarah Kredentser   MD, CCFP, FCFP
Chris Randell   MD, CCFP, FCFP
Claude Renaud   MD, CCFP, FCFP,
Director, Department of
Professional Affairs, CFPC
Christine Wackermann   Liaison, Health Policy Coordinator,
CFPC

❖

Rena Mendelson   MS, DSC, RD,
Associate Vice-President, Academic,
Ryerson Polytechnic University

Anne Lindsay   Nutrition Editor,
Canadian Living

❖

We are grateful to the following for permission to adapt
their material:

B.C. Ministry of Health and Ministry Responsible for Seniors,
Canadian Cancer Society, Canadian Dental Association,
Canadian Fitness and Lifestyle Research Institute, Canadian
Mental Health Association, Canadian Pharmacists Association,
Centre for Addiction and Mental Health, Health Canada,
Heart and Stroke Foundation, Osteoporosis Society of Canada,
Society of Obstetricians and Gynaecologists of Canada,
The Canadian Hearing Society

Contents

Introduction

It's after 11 p.m. on a Sunday night and there are three more acts to go at the Toronto Rock Revival, a raucous reunion of bands who first played in Yorkville in the sixties. The emcee, sporting a long grey ponytail, asks the middle-aged crowd if everyone is having a good time. Much loud cheering.

Then he notes the age of most of the people in the hall, including himself. "It's getting late for us. How many had a nap this afternoon before they came?" he teases. The crowd gives a collective guffaw that makes it clear many have closed their eyes earlier in the day in preparation for a big night out. My husband, Christopher, grins and gives me an elbow in the ribs to say, "Hey, we aren't the only ones."

And indeed, we aren't. We're part of that huge bulge of Canadians moving through the midlife transition a little surprised both by how much in our lives together is the same and how much is changing. Christopher and I don't feel much different than we did when we first heard Lighthouse on vinyl. But of course, we are different. Our bodies are certainly not 20-year-old bodies. Our life view is changing. And so is our family structure. And lately the changes have come thick and fast. Two years ago, when I started writing this book, I didn't know what a night sweat felt like, Christopher didn't know what his blood pressure numbers were, and neither of us knew how we would feel as we helped our eldest pack up for her first year away at school. Now we have intimate knowledge of all of the above.

This book is written for all the couples like us who are manoeuvring through midlife together and could use a road map to the new physical and emotional landscape. You may be in your late 30s, just experiencing the first hint of change signalled by a single grey hair or a subtle difference in your menstrual cycle.

Or you (or your partner) may be in the midst of more dramatic hormonal changes that usually happen to men and women on the other side of 50. Wherever we are on the continuum, each of us needs to understand our own physical changes and the changes our partner will experience. We need to know what will change about sex in midlife and what probably won't. We also need to know how to tweak our lifestyles to maximize our health as we age. Since we eat together, sleep together, and relax together, we can be a positive force in each other's lives – or not.

The information and advice in this book comes from a wide range of sources, both Canadian and international. With the help of two able researchers, Laurel Aziz and Susan Pedwell, I accessed the latest research on menopause, andropause, and sexual health and the best advice to avoid the diseases that become more common with age. The collaboration of The College of Family Physicians of Canada means that the information has been read and endorsed by a panel of family physicians. The material is current and consistent with the advice you'll get when you visit your family doctor. Of course, nothing you read here is meant to replace your doctor's guidance or instructions.

Throughout the book are interviews with couples from across the country who were wonderfully open and honest about how they work through the health and wellness issues of midlife in their personal lives. I have to add, however, that they didn't always say what I expected them to say. Sometimes one partner sounded – at least to my ears – blithely unsympathetic to the concerns of the other. Sometimes their approach to a problem disagreed with expert advice elsewhere in the text. But except for changing details to protect privacy, I made sure their comments were their own. They are real couples working through real midlife issues, and most of us will recognize ourselves in their experiences.

None of us have perfect marriages to perfect partners. We don't always understand each other and support each other, although most of us try most of the time. But what I discovered in writing *Healthy Together* is that the midlife transition is a productive healthy time in our lives, made better by a strong couple relationship. And if you plan to attend any rock concerts, nap first.

Christine Langlois
Toronto, 2000

1

Health Intertwined

Whatever midlife is – and no one agrees – it involves the physical and emotional changes that all of us go through, most of us as a couple.

Men and women in midlife are often compared to teenagers. Like teenagers, we're dealing with hormonal changes and major life changes all at once. But unlike teens we have a couple of decades more experience to help put these changes in perspective. And there's another big difference. While teens and young adults move through their upheavals with a constantly changing cast of characters – parents, friends, roommates, girlfriends, boyfriends, or co-workers – whose influences vary in significance, most of us in midlife have one constant companion, and that's our significant other.

It's your partner (male) who sleeps beside you when you throw off the duvet in a night sweat. He's the one who listens to you worry about how quiet the house will be when there are just the two of you and, in the next breath, calculate how much it will cost to turn a kid's bedroom into a home office. It's your partner (female) who gives your balding head a pat and who listens to you agonizing over whether your knees can take another season of hockey.

Whatever midlife is – and no one agrees – it involves the physical and emotional changes that all of us go through, most of us as a couple. Many of these changes go to the very heart of our relationship. Hormonal changes can affect our sex lives. A decision by one to stop smoking, or to eat less fat, can force day-to-day change on the other. Deciding that you no longer care about that next promotion but that you do care about asking your mother to come live with you involves major negotiations about how you see your future together.

Small physical changes – like being unable to read the fine print on the cough syrup – remind us that we are aging. So do painful life-altering experiences such as the illness or death of a parent. Like everyone else who has ever lived this long, you begin to understand that you're mortal and so is your partner. Your own health and that of your partner can take on much more importance during your middle years, and you may find yourselves in new negotiations with each other about how best to maximize your health together.

Do Married People Live Longer?
Or Does It Just Feel That Way?

Bad joke. But the truth is that marriage is good for you because married people do live longer and are healthier than those who never married or who are divorced. Scientists have been studying the phenomenon since the early 1970s, when American sociologist Walter Gove first published his observations that those who are married have lower mortality rates than those who are unmarried. Married people have the lowest mortality rates, followed by the never-marrieds. Divorced men and women have the highest mortality rates, possibly as a result of the stress of the breakup itself.

Why being married should contribute to better health and therefore a longer life isn't completely understood. One logical explanation is that being married usually improves both partners' financial situation and, in general, the better your socioeconomic status, the better your health is. Marriage may also provide a buffer against the world and the stresses of life, which is the "social support" theory of why marriage benefits health. Being married means, presumably, that you have someone to share intimate thoughts with and to enjoy leisure time with. It may mean you have a wider social network of family, friends, and neighbours. Study after study shows that a social network is an important factor in improving health. In the simplest terms, it may be just as important to build intimacy with your partner as it is to live smoke-free or walk regularly.

Being married also influences strongly the choices you make – whether you wear your seat belt, how much alcohol you drink, whether you eat oat bran for breakfast. This is the "social control" theory of how marriage affects your health. Marriage changes how you behave. Studies of people's lifestyles before and after marriage show that behaviours change for the better. Couples follow more regular routines, eat and sleep more regularly, and live "an orderly lifestyle" as researchers call it. Having a partner to account to for our actions – whether it's how much we drank at the office party or whether we went to aerobics class – gives us reason to make healthier choices. In a Dutch study of the behaviour of more than 116,000 men and women, researchers found that married people were more likely to exercise and eat breakfast and less likely to smoke or drink heavily. Married men were the most likely to be at a normal weight, which, no doubt, drove their wives crazy.

When I told my husband, Christopher, about this theory, I called it the "Button up your overcoat, you belong to me" theory. He said I should call it the "Under my thumb" theory. Funny guy. But he has a point. Wives appear to exert more control over their husbands' behaviour than vice versa. Women are more likely to be the chief cooks and grocery shoppers, for example, so they have more influence on what both partners eat. And women are more likely to be caregivers when someone in the family is sick. They are the ones who make the doctors' appointments, and they're also more likely to dispense health information to their nearest and dearest. The analysis of a small focus group of men in London, Ontario, was reported in 1998 in *The Canadian Nurse*; the men said they got their health information from their wives and girlfriends and from the media. The "social control" theory of why married people live longer also explains why marriage seems to benefit men more than women. The speculation is that marriage is healthier for men than for women because the wives do more to keep their husbands healthy than their husbands do for them.

Men are often accused of ignoring symptoms of illness and delaying going to a doctor. But a large study of Scottish men and women in early and late middle age published recently in *Social Science Medicine* disputes this. When men and women reporting similar symptoms were compared, the two groups were equally likely to go to the doctor. And although men seem less likely to take responsibility for the health needs of others in the family, they're more willing to change their health behaviours based on how they impact on others in the family. In the London study, asked what health promotion strategies would be most effective, in general men responded that they would welcome information about how their health habits and behaviours might impact on their wives, children, grandchildren, and retirement.

Being married is good for the health of both partners, but the quality of your marriage is also a factor in the quality of your health. When men and women report that their relationship is either improving or deteriorating, they report the same for their health – both physical and mental. And when one partner gets sick, there is a corresponding strain on the marriage. A 1994 study reported in the *Journal of Marriage and the Family* made the interesting observation that it's the spouse, not the person who is ill, who complains most of the adverse affects of illness on the marriage. It's the well person, not the sick person, who feels most keenly the loss of the usual shared activities of married life.

Focus on Health Defines Midlife

What's midlife? We're just starting to find out. We understand the developmental stages of childhood and adolescence and we know quite a bit about the needs of seniors, but midlife has been the least studied period of the lifespan. We think we know what we're getting into – midlife crises, the empty nest, menopausal angst – but new research suggests that much of what we believe or have been told about midlife is more myth than fact. The John D. and Catherine T. MacArthur Foundation Research Network on Successful Midlife Development (MIDMAC), an American multidisciplinary research group since 1989, released findings from 10 years of study of 8,000 Americans. The picture these academics drew of middle age was of men and women at the peak of their productivity, in good health, with a sense of control over their lives that they didn't have in early adulthood.

A 30-year-old thinks midlife starts at 40; a 40-year-old says it starts at 50.

Defining midlife by chronological age is a bit tricky. Obviously you can't be sure when the middle of your life is because you don't know when the end will come, although the likelihood is that it will come later than it did a generation or two ago. At its broadest, midlife is from age 30 to 70, with the years from 40 to 60 as the core. But it all depends who you ask. A 30-year-old thinks midlife starts at 40; a 40-year-old says it starts at 50. But age isn't as important as roles in defining midlife. Although we can describe childhood as a series of stages related to age, no real evidence exists for life stages related to age in midlife. You don't work through one stage in order to begin the next. Rather, life events force new roles on you. For example, at 40 it's possible to be expecting your first child or your first grandchild. But since being a grandparent is a midlife role, the moment you become

Talking about . . . facing midlife changes

Ron, 40, a heavy-equipment mechanic, and Martha, 39, a sign painter, have been married twenty years. They live in Wingham, Ontario. They have two children, ages 9 and 12.

Martha: Well, I haven't thought about midlife changes, and I think that's half the secret. Just let them come and don't worry. We're best friends; we'll get through. We'll just take one day at a time. That's all we can do.

Ron: As far as our values go, we see things, not in the same way, but very close. Like I was saying to Martha, it wouldn't matter if the whole thing caved in on our heads. I don't care about the number of cars in the driveway or any of that other stuff – it just doesn't matter. It wouldn't matter if we ended up in an apartment over a gas station in Timbuktu – as long as we're together.

Martha: Laughter – that's important to us. We have a good time. We sit on the porch and have a cup of coffee. We'll talk about our day and we'll just howl. The neighbours must think we're on something. One day turns into the next and, all of a sudden, years go by. That's how we'll get through the next few years. It goes so fast. I think that if you sit around worrying about it, you're wasting it.

Ron: We rent a cottage on Manitoulin Island and we've seen friends there every summer. Then one summer, we heard that the wife had breast cancer and the next thing we knew, in the fall she was dead. They had a couple of little kids. I said to Martha, now that's a problem, not like any of the other stuff.

Life is like a merry-go-round that just goes faster and faster. Our son, he's only 12 but he's huge. He has size ten feet. Where's my baby?

one defines when *you* are in midlife. Other major life events that define middle age are the kids leaving home and the death of a parent.

Margie E. Lachman, a professor of psychology at Brandeis University and one of the MIDMAC researchers, says that in midlife we are living in the middle between the young and the old. "According to our research, midlife appears to be a time to look back and a time to look ahead, a time to ask how things are going and what is left to do," she writes. Young adults focus on the future, elderly adults look primarily to the past, and those of us in midlife look to both the past and the future, aware that we are halfway through our lives.

In midlife we often have responsibilities for both young and old. Midlife is a bit like that game of "monkey in the middle" – you're always trying to catch the ball tossed your way by the generations on either side. Just this afternoon I was doing some calendar juggling. I was planning when to take Lorna, our 19-year-old daughter, to her new school to register for her first-year courses and realizing that the only time she could go conflicted with my promised visit to my grandmother for her 94th birthday. A small problem easily managed by moving up my grandmother's visit a day or two but a typical example of the constant tug those of us in the middle feel from the generations behind us and ahead of us who are counting on us. When part of the juggling act includes acting as caregiver to an older family member, the responsibility can put stress on you and your relationship. But the caregiving role may be part of what midlife is all about. In a recent study published in the *Journal of Marriage and the Family* called "Does It Hurt to Care? Caregiving, Work-Family Conflict, and Midlife Well-Being," Nadine Marks suggests that caregiving is an important midlife role (along with the roles of marital partner, employee, and parent). What makes being a caregiver in midlife difficult is that there are so many other competing demands on our time – pressures from work and other family members; the caregiving role itself is not necessarily difficult.

What's more, most of us do handle the added responsibilities in midlife. That was one of the encouraging findings of the MID-MAC research: midlife is generally marked by a sense of control, competence, and productivity. The stereotypes of the 40-year-old sports-car driving, girl-chasing man in the throes of a midlife crisis or the sweat-drenched, slightly hysterical, menopausal woman crying over her empty nest were just not borne out in the research. Less than a quarter of the people surveyed experienced a midlife crisis and only some of those tied the experience to the aging process. For most, a crisis in midlife was an event such as job loss that was not necessarily connected to aging. And as for perimenopause and menopause, just 10 to 20 per cent of women reported severe discomfort in the form of hot flashes, night sweats, or insomnia. Depression was rare. Women who were depressed had either demonstrated a tendency to depression in their younger years or experienced a surgical rather than a natural menopause. Also rare was empty nest angst. Most women and men, presumably, are pleased to have their children launched. And finally the MIDMAC study debunks the idea that women mourn their loss of fertility at menopause. For the majority of women, the fertility issue is resolved when they decide they've had their last baby. And that decision is usually made at least fifteen years before menopause, which occurs on average at age 51. I don't know about you, but I don't know many couples in their early 50s who mourn the fact that they can't have a baby.

Health issues are, however, a preoccupation of midlife, if for no other reason than that we begin to experience reminders that our bodies are aging. For example in your invincible 20s, neither of you cared much about the state of his prostate or even knew where it was. Now you both know its exact location and care deeply about how the little gland is doing. But the MIDMAC group found that when it comes to our health, we may actually be overly optimistic. While the majority of those surveyed said that their health was within their control, only about 25 per cent were getting enough physical activity or following good eating patterns. Fifty per cent of women and about 25 per cent of men admitted that they couldn't walk up a hill quickly without becoming short of breath.

So if the myths of midlife weren't borne out in this most recent research, what are the realities of midlife? Researchers are exploring many theories. The halfway point adds a sense of urgency to life that you may not have felt earlier. Have you accomplished enough? What is there left in life that you still want to accomplish and is there time? Reflecting on your life so far and considering whether you might alter your life course are probably ongoing topics of conversation for both of you. You may also become more concerned with what social scientists call "generativity," the guiding and nurturing of the next generation, or with improving your community. Some researchers suggest that gender roles blend in midlife, that men become more nurturing and women become oriented toward achievement. It's interesting to explore the theories, but each individual and each couple follows a unique path that may have little to do with the overall trends.

While both men and women may become more reflective and questioning in midlife, one part of their life they aren't as likely to question is their choice of marriage partner. As a MID-MAC Director's Bulletin puts it: "Midlife is a time of relative stability in marital status, as most marriages and marital disruptions precede midlife and most widowhood occurs at older ages."

Talking about . . . reaching middle age

David, 37, a financial planner, and Sandra, 37, a homemaker, have been married fourteen years. They have three children, ages 8, 10, and 12. They live in Vancouver, British Columbia.

David: I think middle age is more of an emotional change than a biological change. I'm feeling some of those midlife feelings. I'm starting to become more interested in me and what makes me happy. Our oldest is 12, so we've spent years dedicated to the kids. The vacation we just took [without the kids] was our first. It was wonderful. We're starting to enjoy more financial freedom. Our work is starting to pay dividends.

Sandra: I think the financial freedom is just broadening our lives. We can talk a little more about what to do next because we don't have that financial stress. It's not such an issue to order a pizza or whatever, whereas before it was. We're able to do a little more. In the past, we certainly wouldn't have done the vacation the way we did, stayed in the best place, ate in the best restaurants. The relationship is the same but the pressure is less. We still have as much fun together.

Midlife Marriages: Facing Change Together

If you've followed the traditional schedule of marrying in your 20s and starting a family a few years later, by early midlife you're heading past the ten-year mark of marriage and you are into some very busy years. "Overwhelmed" is the way lots of couples in their late 30s describe how they feel. By late midlife, again on the most common schedule, you're looking forward to more time for just the two of you as your kids gain independence (if not their own apartment) and you gain more control over your lives. But, of course, you can be at various stages along the marriage continuum – just married for the first time, in a second marriage, or celebrating your 25th wedding anniversary. As you think about how the two of you will move through the health issues of midlife, it makes sense to broaden your view and consider where you fit on the marriage continuum. As couples, we move predictably through the stages of romantic love and power struggle to true partnership. (See Love Stages, page 24.)

I don't think you can separate your desire to work toward good health from your desire to work toward a healthy nurturing relationship. If your relationship is still at the "power struggle" stage (and many in midlife are), then it will be tough understanding how to support each other during the hormonal changes of midlife or even agreeing to live healthier lives. If you can't agree on who is to cook dinner – "It's your turn." "No, it's your turn" – then the choice of a healthy meal is secondary.

Psychiatrist Dr. Jerry M. Lewis of the Timberlawn Foundation in Dallas, Texas, has studied couples for thirty years; he says that the state of a marriage is a major factor in an individual's physical and mental health. He distinguishes between a couple's style and the characteristics that need to be present for a relationship to function well. On style, he writes: "Some competent couples have a charged passionate bond, and others present a more

Love Stages

Romantic Love – There are several theories that attempt to explain what makes couples fall in love. Whatever the mechanism for choosing a mate, the first period of a relationship is a wonderful time of being together that makes each of you feel more complete. Individually you feel more alive and energized. Romantic love has even been discovered to have a chemical base. When you're "in love" you may produce more endorphins and serotonin. You're literally on a high. It's a wonderful, pivotal period in a relationship, but it doesn't last very long.

The Power Struggle – It's as if the blinders come off and some of those traits you once found so endearing in each other are now cause for irritation. You may struggle for control over how much intimacy to share, what are the best ways to parent your kids, and even who should pick up the milk. One or the other may feel that some need of theirs should be fulfilled within the relationship but it is not being met. Not enough sex, not enough affection, not enough listening, and on and on. This period may last years, even decades, and relationships can often end during this stage.

True Love – Only when couples let go of the power struggle and begin to work on their communication skills can they nurture their relationship together. With that nurturing comes the joy of a deep and abiding love, the foundation of a true partnership. With some luck and much hard work, you can reach this stage of your relationship at some point in midlife.

even and bland exterior. For some, a vibrant sexuality is present, while for others, the sexual relationship is more peripheral. Some competent couples share a strong emphasis on career; for others, careers are valued not for themselves as much as for what marital and family benefits they provide. Religion is another difference. For some, neither beliefs nor practices are important, while for others, religion provides an important foundation for the marital relationship."

But style doesn't affect two of the intrinsic characteristics of a well-functioning relationship: power is shared; and both partners influence how much connection and how much separation there is. Shared power means that differences are not a source of conflict; they are valued. The general tone of the relationship is optimistic and affectionate, and the partners express feelings openly. Lewis says that for competent couples, problem solving is highly developed, and conflict, though inevitable, doesn't escalate or generalize into other areas of the relationship.

> For competent couples, problem solving is highly developed, and conflict, while inevitable, doesn't escalate.

During the middle years, many couples are working to resolve their conflicts so that small arguments do not spiral out of control. The effort is good for your health. One study reported in a paper entitled "High Blood Pressure and Marital Discord: Not Being Nasty Matters More than Being Nice" involved measuring blood pressure levels during a problem-solving discussion between a patient with high blood pressure and his or her partner. In female patients, blood pressure increased as the exchange became more hostile. Men's blood pressure fluctuated with their own rate of speech. But pleasant or neutral exchanges had no impact on blood pressure. So we might conclude that if you want to do good things for your health, avoid nastiness. And if you want to do good things for your relationship, stay healthy together.

2

Hormonal Changes

As you go through the hormonal changes of midlife together, you may find that you are bewildered by what your partner is experiencing. That's not surprising, since very little has been done to educate men about women's changes or women about men's changes.

When you read through the scientific literature on midlife hormonal changes for men or for women, you can't help but be struck by the bleakness of the language. Hormonal changes are almost always described in terms of loss and decline. Words like *atrophy*, *deficiency*, *depression*, and *dysfunction* appear with regularity. Pamphlets put out by medical organizations and meant for consumers lead off with a bright you'll-be-just-fine approach, then hit you over the head with a litany of problems that you *might* have to deal with as estrogen production in the ovaries slows and stops in women and testosterone production decreases in men.

But if, as we saw in the last chapter, midlife is a time when we feel a growing sense of control, the future doesn't have to be bleak. All of us, men and women, will experience hormonal changes in midlife. Some of those changes may irritate us, surprise us, or worry us. But if what we now know about midlife is true, they probably won't make us miserable or ruin our relationship with each other.

As with each transition in life, the more you know about what to expect, the better. And by now you have a history of transitions to learn from. It may seem juvenile but I think it's worth remembering how you felt as you moved through puberty, the first big hormonal changes your body went through. Even if you were lucky enough to know about menstrual bleeding and nocturnal emissions, you didn't know what your experiences would be. Some sailed through puberty without even a pimple. For a few, it was a hormonal storm of uncomfortable physical changes and wild emotions. And most of us muddled through with some physical and emotional discomfort and a sense of excitement at the new person we were becoming – a new person who was much more than the sum total of his or her hormonal parts.

As you go through the hormonal changes of midlife together, you may find that you are bewildered by what your partner is experiencing. That's not surprising, since very little has been done to educate men about women's changes or women about men's changes. When the North American Menopause Society was contacted for information on what men know or need to know about menopause, the response was "That is a very good question," but the society had no information on the topic. At least when we first learned about hormones back in health class, most of us learned what the opposite sex could expect, too, although not in co-ed classes, of course.

What struck me as I talked with friends about this book and interviewed couples for the case studies was the amount of misinformation people hold as gospel. And much of that misinformation was based on the assumption that their midlife experiences would be the same as what their parents had experienced. Men whose fathers experienced depression in midlife assumed that they would have a similar "midlife crisis." Women whose mothers had a difficult menopause assumed that they would have the same.

While your individual family histories do play a part in what you will each experience, the range of possible experiences is very broad. Better not to make assumptions but rather to gather the facts and to explain openly to your partner what's happening to your body. If night sweats are disturbing your sleep or an enlarged prostate is getting you up every night to hit the bathroom, then say so. Don't just snap at each other in the morning.

What's Menopause for Anyway?

Just as it's important to understand your own personal experience, it's fascinating to consider the meaning of hormonal changes in the context of wider human experience. As I was writing this section, I read a review of Natalie Angier's book, *Woman: An Intimate Geography* (Houghton Mifflin, 1999), which mentioned the grandmother theory of menopause. I just had to check it out. Angier documents the work of anthropologist Kristen Hawkes with the hunter-gatherer tribe of Hadza who live in northern Tanzania. Hawkes's work neatly connects the main reason for menopause to what it means to be human. Hawkes observed that post-menopausal women in the tribe had a positive influence on the reproductive success of their adult children because they took on the responsibility of foraging for food while their daughters or daughters-in-law were busy nursing their babies. It was grandma who made sure that the rest of the grandchildren got enough to eat when mom couldn't. If these grandmothers had still been fertile themselves, they couldn't have taken on this role. In the animal world, no other female primates take on this job. Hawkes suggests, from an evolutionary point of view, that this ability to contribute to the nutrition of the grandchildren may be why women experience menopause and live beyond the end of their fertility. It meant that the children could have longer childhoods and that humans could develop more intellectual capacity. So it's grandmas who created intelligent humans with longer lifespans in the first place. If you're a middle-aged woman, you've got to love it. Theories like this one lift your spirits after you've read one too many medical papers with the word *atrophy*.

First Comes Perimenopause,
Then Comes Menopause

Here's the timeline on midlife hormonal changes for women. It's a long, slow process. To understand it, we need to go back to health class for a refresher on the menstrual cycle. Every woman has a finite number of eggs contained in her two ovaries. Each month an egg ripens within one ovarian follicle; one egg is released at ovulation and moves down the fallopian tube to the uterus.

The body's rhythmic secretion of two hormones, estrogen and progesterone, controls this monthly process. The ripening of an egg within the ovary produces estrogen, which causes, among many other things, the lining of the uterus to thicken. The production of estrogen peaks just prior to ovulation, when the egg is released. When the egg leaves the ovary, the follicle is transformed into something called a corpus luteum, which produces progesterone. Progesterone causes, among other things, the growth of blood vessels in the uterus and activates the system of glands to nourish a fertilized egg. If the egg isn't fertilized by the end of the cycle, the production of both estrogen and progesterone drops, causing the uterus to shed its lining and get ready for the next cycle.

So the production of both estrogen and progesterone is governed in the ovaries. In most women, by the mid-30s estrogen production has already started to decrease. By the mid- to late 40s, the level of hormones may fluctuate dramatically. Then, at the average age of 51, the supply of functioning eggs has been used and estrogen production in the ovaries ends. Menstruation stops completely, and you've reached menopause. You can only be sure of this in hindsight, once you've been without a period for a year. Menopause is confirmed when a woman has not had a period for twelve months in succession and there is not another

medical cause. Your doctor can order a simple blood test for follicle stimulating hormone [FSH] to help determine whether
you've gone through menopause. As menopause approaches, FSH
increases in an attempt to jump-start your ovaries into producing
estrogen. An FSH reading of 30 MIU/mL indicates that you're
probably menopausal.

WHAT'S PERIMENOPAUSE?

The *peri* simply means *around* menopause, so it encompasses the
years leading up to menopause and the year or two after
menopause occurs. It's a period in women's lives that is only now
getting more attention and study. Some experts define perimenopause as just the two years leading up to menopause; others
say it starts in the late 30s, a time when most women begin to
notice subtle but significant changes in their cycle.

Whether you label it perimenopause or not, you'll likely not
have trouble identifying the small differences in your cycle that
point to a lowering of estrogen levels. Some of the noticeable
changes include a shorter or longer period, a lighter or heavier
flow, a lengthening or shortening of the menstrual cycle. Your
periods may not necessarily change radically; rather, they may
take on a slightly different pattern.

Some women may have their first experience of premenstrual syndrome, others may find that their experience of PMS symptoms worsens. Breast tenderness, mood swings, irritability, bloating, and sleep difficulties may become more prevalent in the
week before your period.

Eventually, more erratic changes begin, leading up to menopause. Most women begin these changes in their late 40s, with
menopause occurring at 51. But 51 is the average age. About one-
third of women experience menopause before age 45. So there is

a wide range of years when perimopausal changes can begin. You may miss a period or have very heavy flow one month and barely any bleeding the next. Some women find that the onset of their period changes. Instead of having an hour or two between the first show of blood and the heavier flow, the flow starts immediately. Nearly everything about the cycle can become unpredictable and require you to be prepared for your period to start early, start heavier, or not start at all when you expect it.

Even though your ovaries are still producing estrogen, the amount produced may not be enough to trigger ovulation. You may miss a period but your body will still be in the estrogenic phase, which means the uterine-lining growth continues. Finally, when estrogen levels trigger ovulation, the period can be very heavy. And if your progesterone production is low, the uterus may not shed its lining cleanly so that you experience continuous bleeding. A minority of women experience problems such as flooding or continuous bleeding, which may require medical intervention, such as dilation and curettage. Your doctor may require a uterine-lining biopsy before recommending treatment.

Treatments include progesterone pills to cause regular and complete shedding of the uterine lining or birth control pills to regulate hormonal production. Alternative therapies recommended for menopausal symptoms, such as soy and black cohosh (see Alternative Therapies, page 56), are also recommended for perimenopausal symptoms.

PERIMENOPAUSE AND THE PILL

It may seem counter-intuitive to start taking the birth control pill as your body is winding down its fertility systems. But that's what some experts are suggesting women consider. The pill has proven benefits for alleviating perimenopausal symptoms by regulating heavy, irregular, or painful periods, and helping eliminate PMS, night sweats, and insomnia. (See page 99 for more on effects of the pill.)

Recent research also points to long-term health benefits:

Reduced cancer risk – Your risk of both ovarian and endometrial (uterine) cancer is reduced dramatically while you are on the pill and for at least fifteen years after you stop taking the pill. Your risk of colorectal cancer also may be reduced by as much as 35 per cent.

Osteoporosis – The estrogen in the pill protects you from bone loss prior to menopause so that your bones are strong enough to endure the period of more rapid bone loss during menopause.

THE HOT FLASH

Long the butt of jokes (by women as well as men), the hot flash is one of the most common symptoms of perimenopause and menopause. Estrogen plays a part in regulating body temperature, so when lower estrogen levels occur, your body has a hard time regulating temperature. At least 75 per cent of women experience hot flashes, which may occur for up to five years before and after menopause. They may be most frequent, however, in the year after the last menstrual period.

A hot flash usually begins with a sudden warmth on the face, neck, and chest, and possibly sweating. The heart rate may speed up. The flashes last from one minute to one hour. For some, hot flashes can be triggered by stress, spicy food, or alcohol or coffee consumption. Other women don't see any pattern to their flashes. When they happen at night, they're called night sweats.

What they actually feel like varies from woman to woman and from year to year. I've read about night sweats for years – and I

What's Your Menopause Story?

How you approach menopause will be very individual. It will also change as you learn more and talk with other women about their own experiences and their experiences with their partners. I decided to follow the advice of experts who encourage women to talk together frankly. Whom can we best learn from? Just as we share our menstruating, birthing, and sex life stories, so with menopause we need to learn from each other. At my last book club meeting, I took out my notebook and asked three women, ranging in age from 48 to 55, to spill. Here's what they said.

Sarah, the oldest, said she went into "instant menopause" at 51. With some embarrassment, she admitted that she had been slow to discuss the change with her husband, who is several years younger than she is. She immediately took herself off to the doctor for hormone replacement thereapy (HRT). Natural is overrated, she said. There's nothing natural about the birth control pill, after all, and it's a form of estrogen that has revolutionized women's lives. She has tried different HRT products to find what made her feel best. A year or two after she started HRT, she had some vaginal dryness that made intercourse painful. "It felt like sandpaper," she said. Back she went to her doctor, who increased her dose and solved the problem. "That was a relief," she said, "since I plan to have sex until I'm 90."

Mary said she had gone on HRT, mostly to combat hot flashes, but she disliked the way the hormone made her feel. "Yuck, I hated it. It depressed me, sending me round the bend." She was in the process of taking herself off the stuff without even discussing it with her doctor.

She would rather suffer the hot flashes, even though "they're brutal."
She combats them with diet changes – less sugar, alcohol, and
caffeine. "I think menopause is really an attitude. It's all about how
you see yourself, and deal with it."

Madeline said she thought that our generation was handling
menopause very differently from our mothers. "We'll change everything," she said. Her menopausal experiences so far have been triggered by a hysterectomy to remove uterine fibroids. Although her
ovaries are intact, her doctor wants her to go on HRT, but so far she
has been resisting because of the risk of breast cancer, which figures
in her family history. "My physician is downplaying the breast cancer
risk because we [women] have much more risk of heart disease." The
toughest part of the whole experience has been her husband's reaction
to her hysterectomy, which surprised both of them. Before the surgery,
he was quite blasé, but shortly afterward he became very depressed.
The end of *her* fertility made him face *his* middle age. She got them
both into counselling.

always expected they'd be horrible. They'd wake me up, leave me
drenched, chilled, and agitated. And then about a year ago, I had
one. At first I wasn't sure. But, yes, I was wakened out of sleep, and
I did feel warm, although not in an uncomfortable way. It felt as if
I'd just finished a short run – warm, damp, and aware of my body. I
tossed off the covers and my body temperature slowly came down.
And then when I was cooled off, I pulled the covers back up and
fell asleep. I didn't have another one for months and forgot about
the whole experience. Then it happened again, and now they
occur maybe once or twice a week. They do interrupt my sleep
but no more than many other changes in my life – menstrual

cramps when I was 15, nursing babies in my 20s, sick kids in my 30s. For most of us, life interrupts sleep fairly regularly.

I can hear the women readers who have severe hot flashes and night sweats howling at my description and frequency. Once or twice a week? Big deal. For a minority of women, hot flashes are a nasty piece of work. Here's another woman's description, which menopause expert Janine O'Leary Cobb included in her book, *Understanding Menopause* (Key Porter Books, 1996): "I would like every man and woman to have just one of *my* hot flashes! First, a sudden, unexplained what's-the-point-of-it-all feeling that lasts only five or ten seconds. I know that within the next thirty seconds, I'm going to have a hot flash – waves of heat travelling up my body, perspiration breaking out all over and running down my forehead, a terrible feeling of weakness and exhaustion." And this woman experiences this anywhere from once an hour to four or five times an hour!

There's a cultural element to hot flashes. Japanese and other Asian women report fewer menopausal symptoms, including fewer hot flashes. Some speculate that it's because their diet contains soy, which is thought to reduce the estrogen fluctuations in the body. (See Soy – In a Class By Itself, page 128.) Others theorize that because menopause is not viewed as negatively in Japanese society as it is in other societies, the women are less likely to focus on the physical effects.

There are ways to alleviate the effects of hot flashes and night sweats. Hormone replacement therapy (HRT) usually eliminates them by replacing the missing estrogen. (See Hormone Replacement Therapy, page 46.) You can also try alternative therapies to replace or to even out estrogen levels. (See Alternative Therapies, page 56.) Figuring out whether you have any triggers and avoiding those substances or situations can help. So can being prepared by dressing in loose layers that you can remove or add according to your body temperature. You can turn the heat down or the air conditioner up. One woman I know kept a window open all one winter to counteract the building heating system while she was having a lot of flashes. It must have played havoc with the hydro bill but she felt much better.

Vaginal and Urinary Tract Changes

It's hard to know what to believe about this particular change. The medical description of what happens is grim. Basically, because the tissues of the vagina, urethra, vulva, and bladder contain many estrogen receptors, these tissues atrophy once estrogen levels drop. The vagina shortens and narrows, the lining becomes thinner and is slower to lubricate during sex. The urethra is easily irritated, making a woman more susceptible to bladder infections. As a recent article in *American Family Physician* puts it, "All of these changes enhance the likelihood of trauma, pain and infection and all tend to decrease comfort and interest in coitus." The only solution, the article goes on to explain, is for women to take some form of estrogen therapy. Such descriptions might lead you to think that menopause without HRT sentences you to no sex or lousy sex at best.

However, MIDMAC research shows that vaginal dryness and resulting discomfort during intercourse are rarely reported in non-clinical samples of healthy middle-aged women. Women who have regular orgasms have fewer vaginal changes during menopause than women who don't. Other research shows that women in *new* relationships at menopause don't report sexual problems. And finally, a small study done by a researcher at the Yale University School of Medicine, reported in the *Medical Post*, suggested that women on hormone replacement therapy experienced a loss of sexual interest that non-users did not. So while every list of menopausal effects includes "urogenital atrophy," it isn't very clear how this physical change or its pharmaceutical solution really affects most women.

Vaginal dryness, when it does occur, may be misinterpreted by a woman's partner as her loss of interest in sex, or at least in sex with him. He needs to know that that isn't the case. A change in technique or longer foreplay might make her more comfortable, and you both need to acquaint yourselves with the various lubricants that can help. But vaginal changes during perimenopause and menopause should receive the same understanding as you both display when he has a slower response in achieving an erection. They are both physical changes you'll adapt to, not barriers to intimacy. (See So What Happens to Sexual Performance in Midlife?, page 72.)

INCONTINENCE

In some women, the changes to the urinary tract result in other changes such as urinating more frequently, getting up in the night to urinate, or leaking urine when coughing, laughing, sneezing, or doing physical activity like running. About 40 per cent of middle-aged and older women are affected by incontinence to some degree and about half of them experience problems at menopause. However, declining estrogen alone is not usually the cause. Weight gain, inactivity, caffeine and alcohol consumption also contribute to incontinence. Pregnancies and vaginal deliveries may have weakened the muscles of the pelvic floor, which can result in a leaky bladder. Although the problem usually corrects itself after pregnancy, it can resurface at menopause.

If you're experiencing a leaky bladder, your first move is to start Kegel exercises (and if you've been pregnant and had leaking problems, then start practising Kegels even before you notice any problems). The bladder control system is made up of muscles. By repeatedly tightening and relaxing these muscles, you will improve your bladder control. Kegel exercise can cure more than half of leaking problems if done correctly and consistently. (Is there anything that a little exercise can't fix?) To tighten your pelvic muscles, pretend you're holding back from urinating. Hold those muscles tight for 5 to 10 seconds, then relax. The Canadian Continence Foundation recommends doing the exercise 12 to 20 times (with a 10-second break between contractions). Do three sets of 12 to 20 per day. You should notice an improvement within a few weeks. Once you've regained strength, practise every other day to maintain it.

In a recent article in a Canadian Physiotherapy Association newsletter, physiotherapist Chantale Dumoulin of Université de Montréal outlines an exercise program directed by a physiotherapist that is very effective in helping women with more serious problems to regain bladder control. One way of strengthening the pelvic floor muscles is electrical stimulation; the patient inserts a small device into her vagina, painlessly stimulating and strengthening muscles needed for urination. The patient also does other exercises, especially the pelvic tilt, to improve her abdominal strength, which can indirectly strengthen the muscles of the pelvic floor. To learn about these exercises, ask your doctor for a referral to a physiotherapist or contact a physiotherapist directly.

Discuss these other treatments for incontinence with your doctor or a physiotherapist:

❖ biofeedback, which lets you feel how muscles are contracting, so you can be sure you are contracting the right ones
❖ vaginal cones, which are inserted into the vagina and held in place by muscle contraction, to help identify and strengthen appropriate muscles during Kegel exercises

* medications, including hormone replacement therapy, although it's not clear whether HRT alone will prevent or improve incontinence
* implants of collagen, Teflon, or autologous (your own) fat into the area surrounding the urethra to make the urinary passage thicker
* surgery to reposition the bladder and urethra.

PREVENTING BLADDER INFECTIONS

For some women, urinary tract infections become more frequent with age. The most common symptoms are an urgent need to urinate, urinating more frequently, a burning sensation when urinating, and cloudy or bad-smelling urine. Other symptoms are pain around the bladder area and blood in the urine. Your doctor will test your urine for the presence of bacteria; if you have a bladder infection, your doctor will prescribe a short course of antibiotics, which will quickly clear it up.

Most urinary tract infections occur because bacteria from feces make their way to the urethra and up into the urinary tract. Women have ten times more urinary tract infections than men because they have a shorter distance between the anus and the urethra than men do. To prevent urinary tract infections, take these precautions:

* Urinate after intercourse to flush bacteria out of your urinary tract.
* Drink lots of fluids to flush bacteria out of the urinary system regularly. Drinking cranberry juice, in particular, may help.
* Wipe yourself from front to back after using the toilet.
* Urinate promptly when you feel the urge. Don't postpone.
* Wear cotton underwear, which allows for air circulation.

Mood Swings

Are they part and parcel of menopause or not? Nobody is sure. A major Australian study of middle-aged women, the Melbourne Women's Midlife Health Project, looked at the relationship between mood and menopause in 2,000 women between the ages of 45 and 55 in 1991. Only a small number of women reported being in a bad mood often. The two years after menopause were the worst for low mood, but the dip was temporary; after the two years, women reported their moods were back to normal. In another study, a Gallup poll released by the North American Menopause Society, 51 per cent of American women polled said they felt happiest after menopause compared with earlier decades. Women with partners experienced fewer mood changes than women without partners.

Fifty-one per cent of American women polled said they felt happiest after menopause compared with earlier decades. Women with partners experienced fewer mood changes than women without partners.

Although some experts believe that lower estrogen levels mean lower moods, most scientific studies now suggest that one's mood fluctuates more because of middle-age issues – stress, role overload, fears of aging, and health concerns – than because of estrogen levels. (See Chapter 8, Stress and Depression.)

Menopause and Osteoporosis

There are the short-term discomforts that may or may not affect you during perimenopause and menopause. Then there are the long-term health effects of living with a lower estrogen level. Unless you've been living on another planet for the last 10 years, you know that a woman's risk of osteoporosis and heart disease increases after menopause, and that a lower level of estrogen is partly to blame.

Osteoporosis is a bone disease that affects one in four women and one in eight men over 50. In someone with osteoporosis, bones become porous, thinner, and brittle. The most serious effect of the disease is that it greatly increases your risk of bone fractures, usually to the wrist, hip, ribs, or spinal vertebrae. A broken bone, especially a broken hip that requires surgical repair, can have a major negative impact on mobility and quality of life, particularly for a senior. Osteoporotic bones can be so fragile that they may crumble with the slightest pressure, which can be painful and immobilizing.

Prevention is the route to go. Adequate calcium intake, not smoking, and getting adequate weight bearing exercise can all contribute to maintaining strong bones. In most women, bone strength peaks at about age 20 and remains stable until about age 35. Then, our bones gradually lose density and get thinner. In women, bone density decreases rapidly after menopause as a result of the drop in estrogen levels. According to the Osteoporosis Society of Canada, during the 10 years after menopause, a woman can lose 2 to 5 per cent of her bone density every year. The society has written guidelines on HRT to include these specific recommendations:

❖ Women entering menopause who also have several other risk factors for osteoporosis should consider taking hormone therapy as a preventive measure against postmenopausal bone loss. Postmenopausal osteoporosis is best prevented if hormone therapy is begun at the time of menopause and continued for a minimum of ten years.

❖ Women who have an early or surgical menopause should start hormone therapy immediately and continue until the average age of menopause. At that time, a decision can be made whether to continue this therapy.

❖ Hormones may be started when a woman is in her 40s and showing signs that she is beginning to lose bone density, especially if she has several risk factors for osteoporosis and her bone density tests reveal low bone mass. Although her hormone levels will fluctuate, she will continue to produce her own estrogen. Therefore, it's important that hormone therapy be tailored to the individual and carefully monitored during this time.

❖ Hormone therapy is an effective treatment for osteoporosis, even if a woman is many years past menopause.

Menopause and Heart Disease

Medical experts have been pounding home the message that estrogen protects women from heart disease, which is the leading cause of death in women in Canada. Although women before menopause have less risk of heart disease than men do, their risk rises quickly after menopause so that by age 65, women have the same risk. Heart disease is also second only to joint and bone disease in the limiting of activities and independence of sufferers. Some studies have shown that women who take HRT have only half as much heart disease as women who don't take it. While there is good evidence of HRT's benefits in reducing the risk of heart disease, the benefit is not so clear for women who already have heart disease. A study released in 1998 showed that women with heart disease who took HRT had higher rates of unstable angina than women not on HRT.

After reviewing the science, the Heart and Stroke Foundation recommended that "all women who are menopausal, post-menopausal, or approaching menopause discuss hormone replacement therapy with their personal physician." However, the foundation doesn't go so far as to say that all women should use HRT, pointing out that there are still gaps in the research evidence. Reports from several large clinical trials should be available in the next couple of years, and they may shed more light. It is known, however, that estrogen benefits the heart by:

❖ lowering the level of "bad" cholesterol in the blood (low-density lipoprotein, or LDL) and increasing the "good" cholesterol (high-density lipoprotein, or HDL).
❖ helping the walls of the blood vessels to relax, improving blood flow to the heart.
❖ reducing certain blood clotting factors.
❖ reducing the tendency to put on weight, especially around the waist.
❖ reducing insulin resistance (insensitivity to insulin).

Hormone Replacement Therapy (HRT)

For many women the decision whether to use hormone replacement therapy (HRT) has become very difficult. In fact, very few postmenopausal women – about 10 to 15 per cent – take HRT long-term. There are too many side effects and too many questions. Is HRT the fountain of youth that will protect you from the misery of menopause and the ravages of time? Is it yet another dangerous estrogen experiment unleashed on women by the powerful partnership of the medical establishment and the pharmaceuticals? Is it a sin against nature? Does it cause breast cancer?

It's probably worth stepping back and putting the current debate into some historical perspective. Hormone therapy has been prescribed to women since the 1960s as a treatment for the effects of the hormonal fluctuations of menopause. When first prescribed, it contained estrogen alone and early reports were very positive. The therapy effectively eliminated hot flashes, sleep disturbances, urinary tract problems, and vaginal dryness. Women complained of few side effects. Then came the bombshell. Research began to reveal that after ten years of use, estrogen replacement therapy, or ERT as it was called, increased women's risk of endometrial cancer by eight times. Many women quickly went to their doctors to find out what to do about their medication.

In the 1960s, at the same time as women of our mothers' generation were trying to decide who to believe after the fiasco of ERT, younger women were learning that the early high-dose estrogen birth control pills they were taking were connected to a higher incidence of strokes. It's not surprising, then, that most women today distrust information given to them on the benefits of estrogen.

The solution to the ERT scare was to add progesterone to the mix. It alleviated the endometrial cancer risk but it also caused nuisance side effects that, for many women, were as bad as the menopausal effects they were taking the drug to relieve.

However, after thirty years of research, more and more long-term benefits of HRT have been recognized:

❖ It reduces the risk of heart disease.
❖ It reduces the risk of osteoporosis.

❖ It reduces the risk of colorectal cancer.
❖ It reduces wrinkling.
❖ It may lessen age-related memory loss.

And along with these benefits, there is still the risk of cancer. Now the major concern is breast cancer. The Society of Obstetricians and Gynaecologists of Canada, reporting on a review of all the major HRT studies, concludes that there is no increased risk of breast cancer in the first five years of taking HRT. After five years, the risk increases slightly. After ten years of HRT use, 51 women out of 1,000 will develop breast cancer, compared with 45 out of 1,000 women who have never taken HRT. After five years without HRT, this added breast cancer risk is eliminated.

In one study, 7 out of 10 women said they wouldn't take HRT because of fear of breast cancer. Our fear of breast cancer is fuelled by many factors. Unquestionably we are afraid because breast cancer is a potentially fatal, disfiguring disease. But also because of the efforts of many individual women and organizations, breast cancer research and treatment has received much-deserved attention. The downside of this is that the disease has been so much in the news of late that many women may have overestimated their risk of getting it. In a recent issue of the University of California at Berkeley *Wellness Letter*, the issue of risk was described this way: "Heart disease kills more American and Canadian women every year than all cancers combined. If you are trying to sort out your chances of dying of a heart attack versus breast cancer, remember that the incidence of heart disease among women age 45 to 54 is similar to that of breast cancer, but with increasing age, heart disease becomes far more prevalent. Deaths from heart disease exceed those from breast cancer at all ages over 45."

Many big-name medical organizations have decided that the benefits of HRT far outweigh the risks and side effects. Organizations such as The Society of Obstetricians and Gynaecologists of Canada, The North American Menopause Society, the Heart and Stroke Foundation, and the Osteoporosis Society of Canada all have policies favourable to its use. They either recommend that all women take HRT at menopause or that they consider it in discussion with their doctor.

THE DEBATE

If you're at the age when you need to decide about HRT, then you've probably had to make other hormone decisions in your lifetime, including whether or not to take the birth control pill. Deciding whether to take the pill was, at one time, fraught with similar moral and medical dilemmas. The pill interrupts the natural process of women's fertility. It also has had risks attached to it – particularly the early high-dose estrogen version of the 1960s and 1970s. But the pill gave women control over reproduction and the freedom to have sexual lives separate from the responsibility for procreation. It has caused a revolution not only for women, but for men and all of society. The gains women have made in the last thirty years in equality with men in employment and in family life could not have happened without the birth control pill.

Some women look at HRT as having the same potential to revolutionize women's lives by turning back the clock of aging. Beyond the bonus of fewer wrinkles is the possibility of much less disease and longer lives. If the medical promise is true, what would being age 55 or 65 or 75 be like with a lower risk of debilitating illness? What more could be accomplished and how much more of life could be enjoyed by a more healthy, active army of older women?

But on the other hand (and you need about five hands for all the sides of this argument), some women argue that menopause is a natural stage in women's lives and should not require medical intervention in the form of drugs. Why should every stage of women's reproductive lives be medically managed in ways that may benefit doctors and pharmaceutical companies, but not necessarily benefit women? If you've ever argued for the benefits of natural childbirth, say, you'll recognize the themes of this argument. Certainly, many women refuse to accept the labelling of postmenopausal women as "estrogen deficient" and in need of medical correction. Others point out that women should be encouraged to make appropriate lifestyle choices rather than to take a medication to reduce the risk of disease.

And, finally, some women are opposed to how one hormone replacement is manufactured. Premarin, the most commonly used form of estrogen, is a conjugated equine estrogen, which contains estrogen that comes in part from the urine of pregnant mares. Much of the urine is collected from horses in Manitoba, Saskatchewan, and Alberta and the estrogen is extracted at a plant in Brandon, Manitoba. Some consumers object to this use of horses as a violation of animal rights.

THE SIDE EFFECTS

Even if you've decided to try HRT, if you're like most women, you'll last about a year and then stop. While women have a variety of reasons for refusing to try HRT, they have one main reason for stopping it once they've started. They don't like the side effects, particularly vaginal bleeding. It is the progesterone component of HRT that triggers the sloughing of the uterine lining, and that is responsible for the vaginal bleeding and most of the unpleasant PMS-like side effects. Some women experience bleeding once a month; others experience breakthrough bleeding that can occur at any time. Other common side effects include headaches, sore breasts, nausea, fatigue, and skin irritation (when the medication is delivered by a transdermal patch). Some women also experience weight gain, although doctors point out that weight gain is part of menopause and may have other causes. Progesterone may also negate some of the benefits of estrogen on the heart.

In order to avoid the side effects, most women who *do* stay on HRT stop taking the progesterone component either on their own or with their doctor's knowledge. But in doing so, they run an increased risk of endometrial cancer, if they have an intact uterus.

Rather than eliminate progesterone altogether, some women opt to take progesterone every three months to cause a withdrawal bleed to shed the endometrial lining. Women with intact uteruses who do take estrogen without progesterone should report any irregular bleeding and be evaluated frequently for a buildup of the endometrial lining, both of which can be indicators of cancer. The lining thickness can be measured with a vaginal ultrasound.

MAKING YOUR HRT DECISION

First of all, don't treat the decision lightly. Women will often joke among themselves about whether to take HRT but, in fact, it may have a long-term impact on your health. Talk to your doctor about your risk factors for various illnesses and how HRT might affect those risks. Sort through your moral dilemmas if you have any.

Talk to your partner about your choices. You may discover he knows very little about the risks, benefits, and side effects of hormone replacement therapy. Be prepared to fill him in (or ask him to read this section) and get his feelings on the topic. Just as you discuss plans with female friends, have the same discussion with your partner. It's your decision, of course, but how you handle your menopause should be something you discuss together.

Talking about . . . menopause

Betty Lou, 53, a store clerk, and Jake, 50, a restaurant owner, have been married twenty-seven years. They live in Toronto and have two daughters, ages 19 and 24. Betty Lou experienced her first signs of perimenopause about five years ago, and when they were interviewed, she hadn't had a period for six months.

Betty Lou: I always think it's the same as being pregnant. It's going to happen and then it's over. It's not an illness. The mood swings are worse than anything. And nobody has answers for that. The other thing that throws me is being tired. The hot flashes don't bother me. They don't seem to happen during the day. They only happen at 10 o'clock at night, and sometimes during the night but not every night. In talking to my sisters, they all tell me I have it really easy and that they've had a harder time. Everybody experiences something different. I find it very difficult to talk about with people [other than her sisters]. It's the same thing as asking "Did you have sex in high school?" It's something that you don't talk about. Even though it's supposed to be all open and out there, people don't feel comfortable talking about it, and I don't understand that.

Jake: I didn't think it would be so severe. I thought it would be less of a big deal than it is, for some reason. That's probably a male thing. I've taken these steps in life pretty well for granted. They're going to happen and there's no point in crying over them or lamenting or celebrating really. It's just what happens. I think Betty Lou is more willing to make an emotional issue out of it than I am, although I don't know if she did or not. Maybe she did and that's one of the reasons that we argue even today – because that's something I simply don't recognize and she does, and she's thinking

I should be understanding of how she feels, and I don't have a clue. That's the stuff that causes all these misunderstandings in marriage. One party thinks the other should know something and the other party simply doesn't know – whether they should or not. [Laughs]

Betty Lou tried hormone replacement therapy but didn't like how the medication made her feel. Jake also agreed that the pills made her moods more erratic.

Betty Lou: I don't like taking pills, and the thing that bothered me was that nobody would listen to me about that. Was there some other way I could do this that I didn't have to take medication? The only way I could get that information was by reading. Nobody knew the right answer, so I decided the best thing to do was not to take it [HRT]. I felt instantly better after stopping. I think as far as stopping taking the hormones, it was both of us who made the decision. Right, Jake? We talked about it.

Jake: Yeah, we talked about it and I concurred. I've never said to Betty, "You must stop doing that" on any issue. And certainly that didn't happen here. At the same time, I told her that I thought if she stopped taking the pills things might be a little easier on her. I think I said that.

Betty Lou: I think having teenage daughters and being menopausal is a bit crazy. [Laughs] It was hard to talk to them. I used to try to tell them what was going on but they were at the age when they didn't care about my emotional being. I think that's normal. And we'd all have our periods at the same time.

Jake: Imagine what it was like for me. [Both laugh]

Find out everything you can about the various forms of HRT. The medication can be administered by pill, transdermal patch, creams or gels, and injection. Premarin, containing conjugated equine estrogen, is the most commonly prescribed form of estrogen. It's also the most commonly dispensed prescription drug in the country. You also have a choice of HRT that contains estrogen synthesized from soybeans. A less expensive form of HRT contains conjugated estrone sulfate (CES). This drug is often substituted for Premarin. In some provinces, pharmacists are obliged to offer you a lower-cost alternative. And if you're on a government-assisted drug plan or certain employee health plans, your only choice may be CES. Some women notice different side effects depending on the form of HRT they are taking. If you notice a change in side effects, or new side effects, check to make sure you haven't unwittingly accepted a different form of HRT prescription.

Be willing to try different products before you give up because of side effects. Some women have good luck with a plant estrogen; others feel best on Premarin. Others prefer the patch or cream rather than pills; still others have the most success with HRT injections. Your doctor may need several tries before she finds the right product for you.

Evaluate your use of HRT in five-year increments. This makes sense because risk factors change. Breast cancer risk increases slightly after five years of HRT use; heart disease risk increases more dramatically for a middle-age woman over the same five years. Don't look at HRT as an all-or-nothing proposition. You can decide to take it to alleviate menopausal effects, such as hot flashes. You can decide to take it later for heart and bone benefits. And you can stop taking it at any time.

And finally, watch for the results of several long-term studies, which may shed more light on the effects of long-term use of HRT. As one friend of mine said, "At 45, I hope I have a few more years before I have to decide about HRT. By that time, we'll know so much more."

SELECTIVE ESTROGEN RECEPTOR MODULATORS (SERMS)

A new class of drugs called selective estrogen receptor modulators (SERMs) gives postmenopausal women another option to choose for protection against osteoporosis and heart disease. The new drugs, which include raloxifene, mimic estrogen's effects on some body tissues while blocking its effects in other areas. They are designed to have a positive estrogen-like effect on the heart and bones, but they are blocked from having an estrogen-like effect on breast tissue.

SERMs appear to have an effect similar to (although not as beneficial as) estrogen on the heart and bones, but without increasing the risk of breast cancer. However, since these are new drugs, the research does not yet include the results of long-term clinical trials.

The first SERM approved in Canada for the treatment of a postmenopausal disease is raloxifene hydrochloride, under the brand name Evista, which was developed by Eli Lilly and Company. Raloxifene is approved for the prevention of osteoporosis. It has been shown to increase bone mass by 1 to 3 per cent. Raloxifene may also help prevent heart disease by lowering levels in the blood of "bad" (low-density lipoprotein, or LDL) cholesterol without affecting "good" (high-density lipoprotein, or HDL) cholesterol. However, raloxifene has no effect on menopausal symptoms such as hot flashes; in fact, possible side effects include hot flashes. Raloxifene is now being studied as a possible breast cancer prevention drug.

Another SERM, tamoxifen, has already been approved in the U.S. to treat breast cancer and is being studied for cancer prevention. It works by blocking estrogen activity in the breast. It has the potential to cut breast cancer risk in half for women at high risk for the disease. However, tamoxifen has been linked to a slight increase in the risk for endometrial and colon cancer as well as an increased risk of blood clots that may lead to stroke. Tamoxifen also has possible side effects very similar to menopausal symptoms, which include hot flashes, irregular menstrual periods, vaginal discharge or bleeding, and skin irritation around the vagina.

It makes sense to discuss SERMs with your doctor, but you would be forgiven for feeling a little overwhelmed by the growing variety of treatments available for diseases you may not have yet and may never have.

EXERCISE FOR COUPLES

Women who are physically active have fewer hot flashes than women who are sedentary. Exercise also improves mood and the quality of sleep and reduces the long-term risks of heart disease and osteoporosis. Your program of physical activity *should* include aerobic activity such as walking or running; resistance exercise such as weight training; and stretching. (See Chapter 6, Exercise for Body and Mind.) But if all you can manage is to head out for a brisk walk after dinner some nights, then do that. And take your partner with you. Lots of couples find that menopausal changes are a wake-up call to both to get more active.

ALTERNATIVE THERAPIES

If you've decided on a menopause without hormones, you may be interested in what alternatives are available from naturopathic medicine. Several herbs and vitamins are recommended to relieve hot flashes and vaginal dryness. But Dr. Anthony Godfrey, a naturopathic doctor practising in Toronto, cautions women not to try to treat symptoms in isolation. The principle of holistic medicine is that each person is unique and treatment involves the whole person. Consulting with a naturopathic doctor who will look at your diet, sleep patterns, and exercise habits and recommend suitable herbal remedies is more valuable than looking for a "magic bullet" pill, Godfrey says.

Maja Seidl and Dr. Donna Stewart, a professor in the faculty of medicine and chair of women's health at The Toronto Hospital, reviewed the scientific literature on common alternative treatments for symptoms of menopause. They concluded that the strongest evidence pointed to the use of soy in the diet for reducing menopausal symptoms and for protecting bones and the cardiovascular system. They couldn't find any evidence for the usefulness of any other complementary remedies, such as oil of evening primrose.

However, recently The Society of Obstetricians and Gynaecologists of Canada stated that it had gathered enough evidence for the use of four naturopathic remedies to suggest that they might be useful. They are:

- ❖ black cohosh for hot flashes and vaginal dryness
- ❖ valerian for anxiety and as a sleep aid
- ❖ ginkgo biloba for memory lapses
- ❖ St. John's wort for treatment of mild to moderate depression.

Andropause

Our understanding of how men are affected by the hormonal shifts of midlife is shallow compared with the depth of knowledge

Talking about . . . andropause

Sam, 50, a business executive, and Susan, 47, an actress, have been married twenty-one years. They live in Toronto, Ontario. They have no children. When Sam became impotent, he left Susan. He was eventually tested for low testosterone and was placed on testosterone replacement therapy. Both he and Susan feel that Sam experienced a difficult andropause although their view wasn't supported by some doctors.

Susan: When we were searching for an answer to what was wrong with Sam, there was huge resistance in the medical community to acknowledging or even putting a name to this andropause. My own psychiatrist was seriously doubtful that there is anything like a true male menopause. Our family doctor, who eventually sent him to a specialist, took his blood level and said, "Well, your testosterone looks fine to me." She read it one way and the urologist read it another way. Just because one doctor is resistant, don't stop there and think that you're OK. Find someone who will accept the challenge of looking deeper.

Sam: The reason why male health centres have grown up is precisely because as our generation ages, there's a whole group of us who are having these sorts of problems. What Susan says is right – go to a specialist who understands this issue.

Susan: He was doing things that were totally out of character. And not just in my judgment. Everybody was saying that he was a stranger. It was very, very strange.

Sam: I didn't realize it had happened to me. I began to recognize it when I went on the testosterone therapy. After I started taking it, I realized that my personality had changed in the couple of years leading up to this whole episode. I had become emotionally unstable. I would cry at just about anything, and I had become forgetful. It had become a bit of a joke. Since I've gone on the testosterone, it's like I'm ba-a-ack.

I realized at that point that I had totally screwed up my life over what was, in fact, a medical issue. Susan and I began to talk and we got into counselling with a couples therapist. As a couple, we began to deal not just with the immediate problems in the marriage, but with issues that were decades old. We're a success story. We're back together. I'm 100 per cent, physically and mentally.

we now have about women. In spite of an explosion of books and products aimed at helping men deal with andropause, or "male menopause," much is still unknown about how testosterone levels change as a man ages and how the changes may affect his health. Men are now faced with much the same dilemma women face in menopause: how much to alter the natural process and what's a normal change compared with a medical condition that needs fixing.

To understand this hormonal story, let's revisit health class. As you recall, during puberty, a boy's testosterone levels increase dramatically. It's the increased testosterone that triggers a major growth spurt and change in body shape – his penis grows larger, his shoulders widen, his lean muscle tissue increases, his voice deepens. In terms of body shape and reproductive ability, testosterone makes the man as estrogen makes the woman. But there is one interesting difference; it's testosterone in both men and women that triggers sexual desire.

Testosterone is a cyclical hormone – its levels fluctuate with circadian rhythms (testosterone is highest early in the morning, dropping during the day, and increasing through the night). It also fluctuates depending on what's happening in a man's life. It's a crass way to put it, but testosterone goes up when he "wins" and down when he "loses." Dr. Art Hister, in his book *Midlife Man* (Douglas & McIntyre, 1998), says a man's testosterone levels fall when he loses a job or even when his team loses a big game! And the opposite is also true. When a man is successful in some kind of competition, whether it's a golf game or buying a new company, his testosterone level goes up. But within this range of fluctuation, testosterone levels stay relatively stable in men until between ages 30 and 50. Then they begin to decline gradually.

Men don't experience the same wild hormonal ride that women do at menopause. Rather, they experience a gradual drop in testosterone and a flattening out of the greater fluctuations they experienced as younger men – not such a big morning jolt of testosterone or the same jump after winning at crokinole. Testosterone production drops about 10 per cent per decade from midlife on. However, reductions in testosterone production can vary from man to man. Unlike older women, who all experience lower estrogen levels after menopause, some older men still have the same testosterone levels as younger men.

Most testosterone is produced in the testicles and circulates through the body in the blood stream. There are two measures of testosterone – the amount of circulating testosterone and the amount of bio-available unbound, or free, testosterone. Most testosterone that circulates in the body is bound to a carrier protein called Sex Hormone Binding Globulin (SHBG) and so is unavailable to the body. A smaller amount of testosterone is unbound, or free, and it is the measure of this testosterone that is considered the most accurate measure of a man's testosterone levels.

Seventy-eight per cent of family physicians and 70 per cent of the general population believe that men experience something similar to women's menopause as they age.

Much research is being done to see how the drop in testosterone at midlife affects men. It's clear that less testosterone doesn't affect fertility for most men at midlife and older. Sperm production and motility do decrease, but even elderly men have sperm capable of creating a baby. However, there are medical experts who say lower testosterone levels cause some of the same effects women may experience during menopause. The symptoms associated with andropause include emotional changes (irritability, mood swings, depression), sleep disturbances, fatigue and lethargy, decreased libido and impotence, and hot flashes. Some experts call this constellation of symptoms ADAM, or "androgen deficiency in the aging male." Researchers are looking at the effect of lower testosterone on everything from osteoporosis to heart disease to Type II diabetes.

At the same time, other medical experts snap back that the changes men experience during these years are the result of many physiological, age-related changes, not just decreasing testosterone. Except for hot flashes, for which there doesn't seem to be much evidence anyway, the other "manifestations" that some men experience in midlife can be attributed to stress, as one group of researchers suggests. Also, because testosterone levels fluctuate with health, lower levels could be the result, rather than the cause, of an underlying illness.

Still, there is some popular support for the notion of andropause. In an Angus Reid poll, 78 per cent of family physicians and 70 per cent of the general population believe that men experience something similar to women's menopause as they age. Dr. Roland Tremblay, professor of medicine at Université Laval and president of the Canadian Andropause Society, says, "We know that andropause is real and that it can be a serious health concern for men – but the good news is that it is also diagnosable and easily treatable."

This is where the discussion gets dicey: men are presented more and more with the option of their own form of hormone replacement, called TRT, or testosterone replacement therapy. TRT is offered with the promise of relieving andropause symptoms as well as perhaps protecting them from such diseases as osteoporosis and heart disease, just as HRT protects women.

First of all, testosterone replacement therapy does have definite benefits for men who have inadequate amounts of testosterone, which is a condition called hypogonadism. In these men, it improves their moods and increases libido. Whether TRT has the same effect on middle-aged and older men whose testosterone is gradually declining with age is not known. Only a very small number of middle-aged men have testosterone levels below the normal range, although their levels are lower than they were when

Testosterone Replacement Options

If you're going to try testosterone, what are your options?

Pills – Testosterone undecanoate (Andriol) is an oral hormonal treatment. Most men notice a change within three to six weeks. Pills maintain the testosterone at a consistent level.

Patches – Testosterone is available in a transdermal patch, like estrogen patches for women. There are two kinds of patches: ones that are applied to the arms, thighs, back or abdomen; others that are applied to the scrotum. Both are changed daily. Some men find the body patches can cause skin irritation. Patches release a steady supply of testosterone to the body.

Injections – Injections are the way younger men with testosterone deficiency are given the hormone. However, with injections, the testosterone level starts off high and then tapers off until the next injection a week or two later.

they were younger. Estimates of how many men are below normal vary from as few as 2 per cent to 37 per cent. But since no one really knows what "normal" is, even these estimates are suspect.

Some studies state that men given testosterone do report improved moods and stronger sexual desire, although stronger sexual desire doesn't necessarily translate into better performance. Testosterone doesn't necessarily improve erections. Impotence in older men may be caused by medications or other medical conditions such as diabetes or high blood pressure.

Although doctors are now recommending TRT for some patients, the long-term effects – both benefits and risks – aren't known yet. No one knows for sure whether testosterone replacement reduces the risk of heart disease, osteoporosis, or diabetes, although there have been some positive indications and several studies are in the works.

What's a more pressing question, however, is whether testosterone replacement increases the risk of diseases of the prostate gland, including prostate cancer. In one study, hormone injections increased the men's level of prostate specific antigen (PSA), which is linked to both prostate enlargement and prostate cancer.

Making a decision about TRT is much the same as deciding about HRT, although far fewer men face the decision. You have to gather all the information you can, talk to your doctor, consider your own personal risk factors, and discuss the options with your partner. The two of you may have opposing views on hormone replacement – he thinks it's a crime against nature, she thinks it should be added to the water supply – but you are dealing with many of the same questions, so search for your individual answers together.

If you're interested in testosterone replacement therapy, discuss it with your doctor, who will do a series of blood tests to measure your levels of circulating testosterone, bio-available testosterone, and the carrier protein SHBG. Once on the medication, be consistent about prostate checkups. Two Canadian andropause experts, Drs. Roland Tremblay and Tibor Harmathy, told the *Medical Post* that men taking testosterone replacement should have their PSA levels tested and a digital rectal exam every three months.

LOOK AFTER YOUR PENIS

While dropping testosterone levels are part of this period in a man's life, they shouldn't be blamed for physical changes that men experience for other reasons. For example, middle-aged men who are unaware of normal age-related changes to their sexual experience may be upset by the fact that they sometimes have only partial erections or that they need more direct stimulation for their penis to get hard during sex.

Penises function best when they are attached to healthy well-cared-for bodies. Because an erection is the result of blood flowing into the penis, anything that affects circulation in the rest of the body can affect a man's ability to have an erection. One way to look at it is that anything that's bad for the heart is bad for the penis. Smoking, carrying extra weight, a high-fat diet, and lack of physical activity all have a negative effect on circulation and heart function. They also have a negative effect on erections.

Knowledge Is Power

You both need to know about estrogen fluctuations, testosterone bio-availability, and why tofu should now be on your grocery list. You need to know what changes are normal for you and what changes are normal for your partner. It's easy to blame every bad mood, every night of interrupted sleep, every sexual encounter that was less satisfying on hormones. You'll both be less likely to do that if you communicate clearly with each other about what you're personally experiencing and what you need to understand about your partner.

3

Sex, for Better or Worse

If sex is important to the two of you at 40,
it will be later, too.

The great unknown for many couples moving through midlife is how the physical and emotional changes will affect their own sexual world. Even if you read every detail of hormonal change and how it affects female bodies and male bodies, you still won't know what it means for the two of you and how your middle-aged bodies give and receive sexual pleasure.

You can't know for sure until you've experienced the changes, of course. But by understanding how sexual response evolves in midlife and by building on the sexual experience you already have, you can continue to enjoy each other physically. Forty-, fifty- and sixty-year-old sex may not happen as often and it may take a little longer. But taking longer doesn't diminish the fun; in fact, it can increase it.

Generalizations (or What Studies Say Happens to Sex)

Earlier studies showed that sexual encounters became less frequent with age. But a more recent study based on the Duke Longitudinal Study on aging, which examined the same people at different ages, found that sexual patterns were much more stable than was earlier thought. Most experts now say that whatever pattern of sexual activity you enter midlife with will likely be your pattern in later life. If sex is important to the two of you at 40, it will be later, too. If sex didn't have a high priority then, then it won't likely have one later.

Talking about ... changing libidos

David, 37, a financial planner, and Sandra, 37, a homemaker, have been married fourteen years. They live in Vancouver, British Columbia. They have three children, ages 8, 10, and 12.

Sandra: My libido has increased in the last year or so. Maybe it's a chemical thing. But as you get older, and you've been together for a longer time, you trust on a different level. It's part of maturing to another stage. You mature to become a teen, then to become a young adult, then you mature to middle age. David used to talk about this possibility years ago when the kids were little and I was tired. He'd say, "Wait till you're 35 – you're going to want it all the time." He couldn't wait. To me that was so far out there I couldn't even imagine it. So here we are. He was right.

David: I thought it was great. But as her libido was increasing, it was as if the tables turned. There actually was a time when her graph line was going up and mine was going down. I never had so many headaches.

Sandra: That's when he was changing careers, so I think it had a little to do with stress.

And middle-aged couples today who began their sexual lives during the sexual revolution of the 1960s and 1970s may have different sexual patterns from couples in earlier generations. Married sex in midlife today is more frequent and includes more variety than it did forty years ago.

Men and women have different perceptions of the role of sex within the relationship. Men tend to perceive sex as a separate component of their relationship – they can have good sex and a bad relationship or vice versa; women connect sexual satisfaction with the quality of the relationship itself. But however they perceive sex in their relationship, only about 20 per cent of couples say that loss of interest in sex is a problem they are dealing with in their marriage.

The Health-Sex Connection

Good health is important for good sex. But good sex might also be a way to promote good health. In *Sex over 40*, a popular American newsletter, the editors compiled evidence that sex boosts your immune system, lowers stress levels, and improves sleep. Sex is so good for you that it may well be considered medicine, the newsletter reported.

The endorphins that are produced in the brain and circulate throughout the body during sex are credited with producing the health benefits. Endorphins are natural analgesics, which could be the reason sex can be excellent pain relief. The release of endorphins is also linked to increased levels of T cells, the white blood cells that strengthen the immune system and fight cancer.

So What Happens to Sexual Performance in Midlife?

This is a loaded question because the word "performance" raises red flags for sex experts. It seems we're all a little too fussed about performance, which can seriously undermine the pleasure we're both giving and receiving. That being said, if you don't know what operational changes to expect, they might throw you, right?

Operational changes in him – The big (or should that be no longer so big?) change men notice in their 40s is that their erections are no longer automatic at the first glimpse of a bare breast, that their erections when they do happen aren't always as hard and take longer to firm up. Men may find that they are not as aroused as they used to be by visual images. They may need more direct stimulation of their penis to produce a solid erection. The changes men experience are likely connected to the gradually lowering testosterone levels but they are universal changes that all men experience and shouldn't be confused with impotence (see Impotence, page 87) or testosterone deficiency.

Men will also find that their orgasms aren't quite as strong and they may take longer to reach orgasm. Men climax and ejaculate in two stages – the first stage occurs when the prostate gland and the seminal vesicles contract, forcing semen into the base of the penis. That stage is the orgasm. Seconds later, ejaculation occurs as contractions in the penis push the semen out. Some older men reach orgasm, but don't ejaculate. Some men find that they don't have an orgasm every time they are aroused. Men also find that their refractory period – the length of time they need to wait before getting another erection or having an orgasm – gets longer. Instead of needing minutes or hours, he may need a day.

None of these changes needs to affect sexual pleasure. In fact, many men find they have more control and are able to come to orgasm when they want to rather than too early for themselves or their partner. And the flip side of needing more direct stimulation of the penis is that the woman can now be more creative about helping along an erection instead of avoiding touching so as not to set her partner off.

Operational changes in her – The main change women notice is that they are slower to lubricate during sex. Particularly after menopause, when estrogen levels are lower, lubrication may take several minutes instead of seconds. A lubricant or saliva can help, as can prescription estrogen cream. It's not clear whether the intensity of women's orgasms changes. Some researchers say there's no change in intensity because there is no diminishing of the nerve endings in the clitoris and labia, which are a woman's most sensitive sexual organs. Others say that the vaginal changes that come with menopause can affect intensity.

Less research has been done on sexual arousal in women, but what does seem clear is that women experience fewer physical changes than men.

The Really Big Changes Happen in Your Head

There are no physical reasons why a healthy couple can't give each other sexual pleasure through midlife right into old age, if that's what they want to do. But emotional and social hangups can get in the way. You may have the misguided viewpoint that your sex life should taper off with age. Indeed, our parents may have acted on that premise. It seems that middle-aged couples in the 1950s had less sex than middle-aged couples do now. Our expectations and the emphasis we place on sexual functioning can affect our actions.

But the inevitable physical changes of midlife can also throw some couples off. A penis that doesn't rise instantly to the occasion and a vagina without its usual welcome sign can scare either one of you or both of you at once. You worry that he or she doesn't turn you on anymore or you don't turn him or her on anymore. What you need is a new technique to accommodate the change. Men who need and want more direct stimulation need to say so. Their partners can learn to stroke and fondle them to firmness. Similarly, women need to say when being touched without being lubricated is not comfortable, and let him get used to applying a lubricant. What some couples may find is that the physical changes they both experience have the effect of taking the emphasis off vaginal intercourse, and that they begin to focus more on oral sex or mutual masturbation.

> **In midlife, sex becomes more of a mutual act of giving and receiving pleasure that may or may not involve either intercourse or orgasms every time.**

Men and women become more like each other as they age. Whereas younger men tend to take the lead in sex and feel responsible for their partner's pleasure, older men look to their partner to provide more stimulation, and women have to take a more active role to help their men achieve erections. Young women often don't have orgasms regularly, but most women become more orgasmic as they get older. Men have many more orgasms than women do in their youth and then fewer as they age. In youth, most men see sex as a physical release first and a sign of love second. In youth, women are the opposite. In midlife, both men and women see sex equally as a physical release and a sign of their love. Sex becomes more of a mutual act of giving and receiving pleasure that may or may not involve either intercourse or orgasms every time.

Sexual Misunderstandings Hurt

Not understanding what to expect from sex as we age can be dangerous and hurtful. If you don't realize that physical changes happen to everyone, you can make the mistake of blaming your partner. A man may think his reduced desire for sex is a reflection of his partner's sex appeal. And his partner may be quick to jump to the same conclusion, deciding that the changes in her appearance that come with aging are the reason his erections aren't as strong as they once were.

Women appear to be more sensitive than men to the body changes they experience. Men may say they regret the body changes that come with midlife whereas women are more likely to use words like *ashamed* or *humiliated*. For some women, added weight, wrinkles, and cellulite have a devastating effect on their self-image. They can't see themselves as both middle-aged and sexual. Images in the media imply that sex is for the young, but not the rest. And women are also very aware of the double standard of attractiveness – that women in middle age are considered less attractive than men are at the same age.

Not everyone feels this way, of course. Both men and women can feel free in midlife from the restrictive definitions of attractiveness that they may have accepted when they were younger. If your body has always looked different from the media images of what's considered attractive, you may have dealt with issues of body image a long time ago and moved on. Some people see humour and humanity in bald heads, rubber tires, and sagging bosoms and aren't the least bit concerned about how others see them.

Middle-aged women who find the body changes that come with age painful can rail against the unfairness of it all – of not having any role models, of the double standard of ageism. But that won't likely change what's on television or in magazines in the near future. The better approach is to change the script in your own head and to create your own images of middle-aged attractiveness. So if you can't imagine your 50-year-old body in the role of lover, find ways to change the script, replacing your outdated view of yourself and your partner with more realistic but sensual images.

In *Women's Sexuality Across the Life Span: Challenging Myths, Creating Meanings* (Guilford Press, 1998), author Judith C. Daniluk describes some ways that women can visualize themselves positively at age 40, or 50, or 60. Going through family photo albums and really looking at people you know or encounter during the day can help you find strong positive images of middle-aged women. Don't look too hard for media images because there are so few that are both realistic and positive. Even older actresses held up as positive role models for middle-aged women are of little help. Many have been so altered by plastic surgery or their images have been so manipulated and computer-enhanced that the natural lines and softening that come with age are eliminated. So you need to look further. Most women can think of someone in their family or at work who embodies for her a woman who is both middle-aged and attractive and comfortable in her own skin.

Here's how Gail Sheehy, in her book about menopause, *The Silent Passage: Menopause* (Pocket Books, 1998), sees this image of the future that each woman can create for herself:

> She is our better nature, with bits and pieces of the most
> vital mature women whom we have known or read about
> and wish to emulate. If we are going to go gray or white,
> we can pick out the most elegant white-haired woman we
> know and incorporate that element into our own inner
> picture. The more clearly we visualize our ideal future
> self, admire her indomitable skeleton and the grooves of
> experience that make up the map of her face, the more
> comfortable we will be with moving into her container.

Many women probably do this without even realizing that it's a body image exercise. I've found myself becoming more observant of interesting, attractive, older women ever since I hit my 40s. Sitting on the subway I assess them: What makes them attractive? An inner confidence? Posture? How they carry themselves? Grooming? How often they smile? And I file the image away in my mind, reminding myself that when I'm 50, or 60, or 70, I want to look like that. It helps – especially when one of them is sitting under yet another Calvin Klein ad for underwear.

By visualizing our own images of beauty and attractiveness at each stage of life, we can counter the seemingly endless parade of young models made to represent "women" in the media images that surround us. Just be realistic. If you're a short 40-year-old with large breasts, don't plan to be a six-foot 60-year-old with a boyish figure!

EXERCISE – AGAIN

If you're sedentary, physical activity can make a big difference in improving your body image and your sex life. We're not talking about exercise to change the way your body looks. After all, self-acceptance is the key to a healthy body image. But physical activity puts you in touch with how your body works and feels. You feel better about what your body can do.

Love Those Bodies

If looking for examples of positive images of midlife helps women, it also helps men. And looking for images of midlife sexuality helps to dispel the idea that sex is only for the young. Clint Eastwood, in the movie *The Bridges of Madison County*, looked his age. Actually, so did Meryl Streep. But that didn't stop the two of them from steaming up the screen. You both need to love your own and each other's middle-aged bodies. Those bodies look different at 40 than they did at 20, but rounder bellies and softer biceps won't affect your pleasure in each other.

Choose sensual ways to pamper yourself – massage, rich body creams, pedicures. These are messages from yourself to yourself that your body is worth making feel wonderful, whatever its shape or size. And making your body feel wonderful through sex is an extension of that thinking.

DESIRE – WHERE *does* IT GO?

If you're a couple in midlife with a few years of sexual experience behind you, you're likely aware of the ebb and flow of your sexual desire. Sometimes it's clear where it goes – it disappears along with sleep when your kids are babies. Other times it just fades away as you realize that you're in a rut – same day, same time, same position, same fifteen-minute routine. Or it goes during hay fever season because your antihistamine kills your libido at the same time as it dries up your nose.

Unlike arousal, which is physical, desire is in the mind. It's what makes you think sexual thoughts and "feel" like it. In both men and women, desire is triggered by testosterone. Low testosterone levels can mean less desire in both men and women. In men, testosterone levels drop through midlife. However, this drop is gradual for most and isn't likely to be associated with a major drop in desire. In women, testosterone is produced mostly in the ovaries along with estrogen. While estrogen levels decrease with age, it's not clear yet what happens to women's testosterone levels. Some researchers suggest that desire may actually increase with age for some women because their testosterone levels are unopposed by estrogen. Women whose ovaries are removed as part of a hysterectomy may notice a decrease in desire.

Although sexual desire tends to decrease with age, there is no physical reason for it to decrease substantially. So dealing with low desire is more complex than slapping on a testosterone patch. Many people with normal testosterone levels for their age still feel their sexual interest waning. Sex therapists say that half the people who seek treatment cite low desire or lack of desire for sex as their initial complaint. They also report that lack of desire becomes more frequent after 40.

If one of you has no sexual desire over a long period of time, you may be dealing with a deep-seated relationship or personal problem that requires therapy. But if you've been together for a while, you probably already know that. What's more common in midlife is the gradual waning of desire. You look at each other over breakfast one morning and realize that you haven't made love in a month and, what's more, you don't even care much. Or only one of you is losing interest and leaving the other one frustrated and worried about what's happening to your relationship.

It's your relationship you should look at first when desire fades for one or both. Money battles, disagreements on how to handle parenting issues, frustration with the split of housework responsibilities can all take their toll on your desire to jump into bed together. To increase desire, you need to work on the underlying issues between you.

Or the problem might be outside your relationship. Stress and depression are the main culprits here. You probably already know that if one of you is dealing with stress at work, it affects your interest in sex. Instead of sexual thoughts running pleasantly through his mind, he's obsessing over how to get his work crew to meet the unreasonable deadline his new boss has set.

If you're dealing with a combination of stressors – you're working too many hours, you have no time for exercise, and now you're worried that your sex life has died – then you're even less likely to *want* sex (even though you may be thinking about it). Again, the solution is to deal with your stress, including getting

Talking about . . . making time for sex

Patsy, 42, an office manager, and Steven, 43, a stockbroker, have been married nineteen years. They live in Mississauga, Ontario. They have two children, ages 12 and 15.

Patsy: My libido has always been lower than his. Over nineteen years, we've discussed it off and on. He's always complaining that I'm too tired. I'm a morning person and he's a night owl. He hits his stride at 10 p.m. [Not making love] is not so much lack of interest as it is the demands of the daily routine and lack of privacy. When the kids were younger, they took a lot of energy. Now they're staying up later and there's no privacy. But when we went on holiday last fall, we were away for three days and I think we did it five times. [Laughs] It was very freeing.

Steven: I don't know whether it was the travel or the relaxation. Normally she is on a totally different schedule than I am physically. But even in your 40s, sex is still a big mental thing for both male and female.

some exercise, which has a major positive impact on libido. One researcher, Carol Meston, then at the University of British Columbia, found that women's arousal levels jumped when shown an erotic film after having done twenty minutes of exercise compared with their levels when shown the film without having done any exercise.

Lack of sexual desire has almost become a given for couples with two kids, two jobs, and two mortgages. The crazy, busy lives most people live are not conducive to relaxed fun-filled sex. And advice to schedule dates for sex can just make some couples feel even more pressured. But letting the daily grind overwhelm your sex life will have repercussions for your relationship. Just as you need intimacy to strengthen desire, so you need sexual desire to strengthen intimacy. When it comes to sex in midlife, the use-it-or-lose-it motto applies. Once you let the sexual flame go out, it can become much harder to re-light. Alex Comfort, in his book *The Joy of Sex*, wrote: "Over 50, the important thing is never to drop sex for any long period. Keep yourself going solo if you don't have a partner for the time being. If you let it drop completely, you may have trouble restarting." Funny how I don't remember coming across that reference when I first read *The Joy of Sex* when it was published in the early 1970s. Or I just skipped it because I couldn't imagine ever being 50! Being 50 and still wanting sex seemed even more improbable.

Staying sexually active is also the best way to keep your "equipment" working well. Men have firmer erections and women lubricate more easily when they have regular sex.

What If Sex Is Now a Memory?

All the emphasis on maintaining sexual activity can mask the fact that many couples stop having sex at some point in midlife. They may stop because of illness that either makes sex difficult or leaves him impotent. Desire may fade and they don't focus on getting it back. Or sex may never have been a high priority and it just eventually disappears off the radar screen.

While maintaining and rejuvenating sexual relationships is much researched and much discussed, stopping having sex is not. Wendy Trainor, a Toronto therapist who specializes in sex therapy, says that in our culture, sex has been elevated to a role of huge importance in marriages. But the range of what is normal in sex is very wide. Some couples are able to get their intimacy needs met in other ways in the relationship. Sharing hobbies, their joy in their kids, and vacations together are all part of intimacy.

"No sex is typically a problem in relationships when there is a discrepancy in the needs of each partner and when the couple's difficulty doesn't get talked about or negotiated," says Trainor. "Problems arise when couples withdraw physically and emotionally from each other, which can make them feel very alone. When they build up walls, that's a problem." But when they find different ways to be intimate, then they can create something new and special. "A lot of women would just like to be held or touched or kissed. Men often say, 'I'm fine. I don't need sex as much.' But what they're really craving is touch and affection as well," she says. "Good communication is the key," she adds.

Honey, I'm Bored!

And you can bet that if you are, your partner is too. Sex in a long-term relationship can blossom into an amazing rich experience. It can also be as dull as dishwater. Again, your attitude to lovemaking can determine the direction of your sex life. You can both see the changes you're experiencing as opportunities (he lasts longer, which is good for both of us) or as problems (he takes longer to come, so he must be getting old).

But midlife can be a time to explore new ways of arousing each other. After all, you're most likely not getting up in the night with small kids. Here are suggestions for revving up your sex life if boredom is what you're dealing with. You don't need to try all these suggestions. Pick out a few that appeal and go for it.

GET IN THE MOOD

- ❖ Exercise for sex. Regular exercise can increase sexual frequency and improve performance.
- ❖ Play music that has an erotic or romantic pull for each of you. Music can establish mood; often associations with previous lovemaking or romance make the music especially powerful.
- ❖ Touch your partner outside the bedroom. Hug, hold hands, kiss, massage one another's necks. Physical affection both in private and in public builds intimacy that carries through to lovemaking.
- ❖ Make your bedroom sexy. Banish the computer and the television or at least close them up in a cabinet so that they aren't so intrusive. Choose bedding that is soft to the touch. Light candles and burn fragrance, such as incense.
- ❖ Talk about sex. Tell your partner what you want or what you'd like to try. Patricia Love and Jo Robinson, authors of

Talking about . . . sex and attraction

Ron, 40, a heavy-equipment mechanic, and Martha, 39, a sign painter, have been married twenty years. They live in Wingham, Ontario. They have two children, ages 9 and 12.

Ron: I'm very lucky in a way. I'm still very attracted to her. I guess that's one of the key things. If you're not attracted, you're not going to make advances.

Martha: I'm sure we've changed a lot since we were 20. We've changed together at the same rate. It's not like one of us got obese and the other one stayed in great shape. We've changed together. Fully dressed, we look in good shape. It's when you take off the clothes that there's a little extra here and there.

Ron: She's a beautiful woman. I guess I'm fortunate. I have a tremendous sex drive. You have to wonder if it's ever going to go away. It sure hasn't gone into any lull yet.

Martha: I can honestly say that up until a few years ago I didn't [have a strong sex drive]. It would be like, oh my God, tonight again? Like, give it a rest. I find that has changed. And it's not just that it's easier to get it over with and get to bed. I'm into it now.

Hot Monogamy, suggest finding the desire or the request within your criticisms. Instead of saying "You never go down on me," say "I'd love it if you went down on me tonight." If you want to change something about your lovemaking, then offer an alternative that begins with "instead of." "Instead of starting to make love lying in our usual positions, let's start sitting up facing each other."

❖ Share your fantasies and take part in making each other's fantasies happen. Although most men and women have sexual fantasies, some people keep their fantasies to themselves and others find the play-acting awkward.

❖ Experiment with reading erotic stories to each other. Watch erotic films together. Men and women often have different tastes in erotica. Find something that's a turn-on for both of you.

❖ Be clear about what your signals are for initiating sex. Some couples just say "Let's make love tonight." Others have non-verbal signals. She puts on her sexy nightgown, not the flannel one. He embraces her in a way that says "I'm ready." Agree on your signals and also on your option to signal no when you want to.

❖ Give each other a sensual massage. Use warm scented massage oils.

❖ Take a shower or a bath together. Soaping each other down is good foreplay.

❖ Buy something sexy for your partner. Men are stimulated visually and, for some, revealing lingerie is a turn-on. It's usually men who buy black teddies and garter belts for women, but there's no reason why women can't indulge their men in silk boxers or bikini briefs.

TRY SOME NEW TECHNIQUE

❖ Warm up slowly. Try an extended teasing foreplay to build excitement.

❖ Don't forget the quickie. Not every sexual interlude needs to be long and leisurely. Sometimes, if you're both willing, a brief encounter is a great release.

❖ Get a vibrator and use it on each other. Women reach orgasm quickly with a vibrator against their clitoris. To heighten his orgasm, try the vibrator on him, on the sensitive spot between the scrotum and the anus, called the perineum, or on the underside of the penis.

❖ Perform oral sex on each other more often. Both men and women say being on the receiving end of oral sex is one of their favourite sexual activities. Not everyone likes to give it. If you're uncomfortable with giving oral sex, figure out what's bothering you. Are you influenced by an old taboo that it's somehow wrong or "dirty"? (Solution: Talk it through together and start gradually when you're comfortable.) Are you unsure of your technique? (Solution: Practise. Your partner will probably be happy to give you pointers.) Do you think it's unhygienic? (Solution: Start with a bath or shower.)

❖ Try new positions and places. Try the woman on top, or rear entry. Even changing your usual side of the bed adds variety. If your family situation allows you the privacy, make love in the TV room after watching an erotic video or on a duvet in front of the fireplace.

❖ Try a different time of day. Some couples start making love in the morning once the kids have moved out and they have more privacy.

❖ Introduce a lubricant into your repertoire and use it lavishly. Use it to augment the woman's natural lubrication and reduce irritation, to lubricate a vibrator, or to make a penis slippery for manual stimulation. Or whatever. Two popular brands available at drugstores are Astroglide and KY Jelly.

ROMANCE HELPS, TOO

❖ Enjoy special meals together. A candle-lit dinner, a champagne breakfast, or a late-night treat can all be a sensual prelude to sex.

❖ Bring your partner a gift. Valentine's Day, birthdays, and your anniversary are great opportunities, but small gifts for no reason heighten closeness.

❖ Make romance a priority. Schedule special romantic occasions on a calendar; that way, months don't go by without time set aside to focus on each other.

❖ Plan getaways regularly. Spend a night or two at a hotel. Escape the phone and your usual commitments and spend time together exploring new sexual frontiers.

❖ Say "I love you." Assuring your partner of your love not only nurtures romance and sexual pleasure but also creates bonds of trust that extend to all aspects of your relationship.

Impotence

Impotence, or the newer term, *erectile dysfunction*, is defined as the persistent inability to obtain or sustain an erection for satisfactory intercourse. It's a major worry of men in midlife, which isn't surprising because it's the most widespread sexual problem that men deal with. The rate of impotence increases with age. Getting older does not increase the risk of erectile dysfunction, but the diseases that may come with age do increase risk. At age 40, about

Talking about . . . impotence

Sam, 50, a business executive, and Susan, 47, an actress, have been married twenty-one years. They live in Toronto, Ontario. They have no children. When Sam became impotent, his behaviour broke up their marriage for a short time until he sought medical help. A combination of couples therapy and testosterone replacement therapy helped them restore their marriage and their sexual relations.

Sam: It began two or so years ago. I couldn't have an erection. Or I'd have an erection and lose it immediately. I panicked and misinterpreted what was happening to think that I had fallen out of love with Susan. I had an affair to see if maybe I just needed a different woman. I still couldn't have an erection. So at this point I was in a blind panic. And not to my credit, I left.

I then had the good sense, at last, to go to a doctor. But by this point, our marriage was in shambles and Susan was heartbroken.

Susan: It came on slowly, but after six months or so, it was clear he was having a problem with sex. We couldn't talk about it because you don't go there. Guys are too sensitive about that. I didn't want to confront him because I didn't want to make an even bigger issue of it. I was quiet about it, just trying to be supportive. Sometimes I'd make a joke, which was probably the wrong thing to do. But we really didn't talk about it and I didn't understand how deeply unhappy he was. I was thinking it must be me. I'm 45 – maybe I'm not attractive to him anymore. Maybe I've gained weight. Maybe I'm boring. And then suddenly, he left. I mean, he just left. And I was heartbroken. I still loved him very, very much. So I had a crisis of self-confidence of my own because the man I had been in love with for twenty years had suddenly decided I didn't fit the bill.

Sam: In the books that I read, the authors talked about how isolated men are when it comes to sexual issues. We're isolated from our partners because men really feel it's our job to perform, and we're isolated from other men because we don't talk about it, because we're ashamed. Books really helped me to understand my own psychology and to get over myself to a great extent.

Susan: Men won't laugh and joke about themselves. It's way too personal. They really have a problem talking with other guys and with their wives about sexual dysfunction. [I guess] they see it as a personal failing.

5 per cent of men are impotent and about one-third have occasional dysfunction. Over age 65, between 15 and 25 per cent of men are impotent and most have occasional dysfunction.

The causes of impotence are complicated and usually include both physical and psychological factors. Only about 10 to 20 per cent of cases are believed to be psychological. In older men, physical causes predominate. In middle-aged men, while physical causes are present, psychological problems such as stress, depression, and relationship difficulties are more significant factors in impotence. For many men, a cluster of interconnected problems – both physical and psychological – cause impotence.

Sorting out what's causing the problem is the first step. As soon as you notice that you are having erection difficulties, you should visit your doctor for a checkup. Don't just assume that impotence comes with age. It doesn't. Impotence can be an indication of an illness and should be investigated. And the longer you leave the problem, the more difficult it becomes to regain sexual functioning. Because impotence is so upsetting to men (and to their partners), and they are so reluctant to talk about it, they sometimes ignore it or assume that it's an unchangeable result of their health condition. But there are many medical treatments for impotence, including the much-touted Viagra, and most men can find a way to maintain their sexual activities if that is what they and their partner want.

Make an appointment with your family doctor and go prepared to describe what's changed, when it began, and whether there is any pattern to the problem. Your doctor will investigate to determine whether the cause of the problem is physical or psychological or both, and may prescribe one of a variety of drugs, including Viagra. You may also be referred to a urologist for further investigation.

Having erections depends on having adequate blood flow to the penis. Any physical condition that affects that flow can increase the risk of erectile dysfunction. Cardiovascular disease, high blood pressure, and other illnesses that cause circulatory problems, such as diabetes, can lead to impotence.

The drugs used to treat various conditions, such as antihypertensives to treat high blood pressure, may themselves cause impotence. Drugs can affect sexual response in men by lowering desire or by interfering with erections or ejaculation. (A few drugs can also interfere with orgasms in women.) Doctors don't always mention these side effects if patients don't ask. But it's important to remember that medication still only affects a small number of men. One study, discussed in the *Canadian Journal of Human Sexuality*, followed 557 hypertensive men between the ages of 45 and 69 who were being treated with various drugs. Less than 10 per cent reported erectile dysfunction after two years and less than 15 per cent reported problems after four years. Prescription drugs aren't the only ones that can affect sexual function. Cold and allergy medicines, particularly antihistamines, have side effects for both men's and women's sexuality.

Most people associate alcohol with heightened sexual activity, but too many alcoholic drinks can also make erections less likely. Heavy alcohol use over time can lower testosterone levels, which results in lower desire. It can also cause a nerve disorder in the penis, called peripheral neuropathy, which permanently damages a man's ability to have an erection.

Smoking, which constricts the flow of blood through the arteries, affects blood flow to the penis. Over time, poor blood flow can cause problems in having an erection.

IMPOTENCE SOLUTIONS

❖ Change habits that may be affecting erectile function. Quit smoking, reduce alcohol consumption, alleviate stress.

❖ Discuss medications with your doctor to assess whether any might be contributing to the problem.

❖ *Viagra* – As the first oral treatment for male impotence, Viagra is a much more effective option for treating impotence than the more mechanical devices on the market. The manufacturer, Pfizer Inc., claims a success rate of between 65 and 88 per cent. Viagra works by blocking the enzyme that interferes with cycle GMP, a necessary component for blood flow to the penis. Erections still require sexual stimulation, making the process more like natural sex than injections, for example, which produce erections with or without stimulation. Viagra comes with some side effects that include flushing, indigestion, headaches, nasal congestion and, more rarely, urinary tract infection, abnormal vision, diarrhea, dizziness, and rash. The reports of deaths caused by Viagra in men with cardiovascular disease have been discounted. However, men taking nitrate medications, including nitroglycerine, should not use Viagra.

❖ *Penis ring* – This works for men who get erections but lose them quickly. An elastic ring is slipped over the base of the erect penis to maintain the erection until ejaculation.

❖ *Vacuum devices* – With this mechanical device, the penis is placed in a tube that is pumped to create a vacuum. This causes an erection, which is maintained by slipping a tension band around the base of the penis.

❖ *Injection or pellet therapy* – Most men don't like the idea of this, but it works, particularly for men who respond well to a diagnostic injection of a drug into the penis to cause an erection. Alternatively, a tiny pellet is inserted in the urethra to produce an erection.

❖ *Penile implants* – These are reserved for situations where all else fails, because surgery to install implants destroys erectile tissue, making natural erections no longer possible. Implants are made of either inflatable material (the pump is tucked inside the scrotum) or semi-rigid material (two bendable rods) to produce an erect penis with a hard shaft but with a soft head.

IT TAKES TWO

Not long ago, nobody really knew the physiology of an erection. Now that the mechanics are clear and there are devices and drugs that can produce erections in men with potency problems, something else may be lost. And that is the understanding that there is much more to sex than a hard penis able to make its way into a vagina. Here's a letter sent to *Canadian Living* after the magazine published a piece on Viagra, written by Dr. Art Hister. Hister, by the way, made the point that not every female partner is thrilled that her mate is using Viagra. A 51-year-old divorced woman, who requested anonymity, wrote:

> I dated a 55-year-old man for seven months and recently broke it off. He was an enthusiastic Viagra user! We had a huge gap in verbal communication – I wanted much more, he preferred a great deal less.... Don't get me wrong – I'm a firm (sorry) believer in sex and sexual intimacy, but the problem for us was his inability to share his thoughts and feelings around that whole sexual intimacy issue. I soon began to feel as if I was a reservoir for his pleasure and that my own needs outside of the bedroom were not being met.... Hugging and holding, touching and kissing are the glue that holds men and women together, and without that, there is precious little.

Treating impotence should involve the couple, not just the man. Your doctor may ask both partners to attend a consultation to give perspective on the situation. In a paper published in the *Canadian Journal of Human Sexuality*, sexual medicine consultant Rosemary Basson suggests that male patients often encourage their doctors to focus on penile function by telling the doctors that their relationship with their wife is fine. However, their wives, when interviewed, often give the relationship a lower rating.

Here's advice that Joan Graham, a registered nurse and the former general manager of the Male Health Centre in Oakville, Ontario, gives to couples dealing with erectile dysfunction. She says both partners need to be involved in treatment and in restoring intimacy and sexual confidence.

❖ Keep the lines of communication open. This is not the time to turn away from your partner. Be open about your erection problems. Say how it's affecting you and ask your partner to share as well. At the same time, talk openly about sex, in general. Share what's enjoyable and look at your situation as an opportunity to learn from each other. Focus on your time for intimacy. Spend quality private time together when you're both relaxed.

❖ Be willing to experiment. You can have intercourse and an orgasm with a soft erection by manually inserting the penis. Or forgo intercourse for a month and stick to foreplay, which removes the pressure to perform. After a month, have intercourse only when there is a firm erection and you're not feeling anxious. Spend time pleasing each other without a focus on erection or intercourse. Give each other a full-body massage.

Contraception Choices in Midlife

It is one of the ironies of the midlife transition that one couple can be cheerfully watching the nest empty while another is deciding whether to have a baby. Some couples are considering permanent contraception. Others are keeping their fertility options open.

You've likely used several forms of contraception at different life stages. After age 35, the big question for couples with children becomes whether one of you should undergo a sterilization procedure or whether you should continue with the birth control method you've been using.

Most couples opt for sterilization once both are sure they don't want any more kids. But it's not uncommon for couples to disagree about when their family is complete and for one or both of you to have mixed feelings. Some experts advise waiting at least two years after the birth of your last child before deciding, so that you're not in the thick of the busiest parenting period. The younger you both are, the more likely you are to regret a decision to sterilize. And if your relationship is in trouble, that is not the time to undergo sterilization.

VASECTOMY

Vasectomy for men involves cutting the two tubes, called the vas deferens, that connect the testicles (where sperm is made) to the rest of the male reproductive system. Sperm can then no longer mix with seminal and prostate fluid to be part of the semen that is expelled during ejaculation. A vasectomy has no effect on a man's testosterone production, erections, or sexual enjoyment. According to the 1995 Canadian Contraception Survey, vasectomy is now performed more often than tubal ligation on women.

The procedure is typically done in about 20 minutes in the doctor's office under local anesthetic. The doctor makes a tiny incision in the scrotum to gain access to the tubes, which are cut and sealed.

In North America, about 20 per cent of men over the age of 40 have had a vasectomy. The best candidates are men over 35 who have more than one child, who are well adjusted sexually, and who are in stable relationships in which both partners are satisfied not to have more children. Although reversal is sometimes possible, vasectomy should be considered permanent because reversal involves major surgery and has a poor success rate.

It's important to realize that sterilization is not immediate. It takes as many as twenty ejaculations for all sperm to clear the man's system. In less than 1 per cent of cases, the tubes can rejoin spontaneously, so ejaculate may continue to contain sperm. Doctors ask men to use contraception for two to three months after the procedure, then to return to have a semen sample tested for sperm before resuming unprotected sex.

What Are the Long-Term Effects?

In the last several years, many reports have suggested that men who have vasectomies are more at risk for atherosclerosis, heart disease, and prostate cancer. After further study, the concerns about atherosclerosis and heart disease have been abandoned. In fact, research out of Oxford University and Harvard Medical School found that men with vasectomies were slightly less at risk for coronary heart disease.

The studies on the possible link between vasectomies and prostate cancer are ongoing. Most show no link; a few show some connection. Some researchers suggest that where a link has been found, it is because the men who have vasectomies are more likely to visit a urologist, to be screened, and to have prostate cancer detected early.

TUBAL LIGATION

Like vasectomies, which seal the vas deferens, the tubal ligation seals the fallopian tubes so that eggs can't travel from the ovaries to the uterus. The procedure is performed under general anesthetic. A tiny incision is made close to the navel and a harmless gas is pumped into the abdomen to make room around the internal organs. A laparoscope is inserted into the abdomen to allow the surgeon to view the fallopian tubes and then a second instrument is inserted to seal the tubes. The preferred method of sealing is electrocauterization, which has the lowest failure rate. Tubal ligation has no effect on hormone production.

Women older than 30 who have the number of children they want, are in a stable relationship and who have no menstrual abnormalities are the best candidates for the procedure.

Tubal ligation is more than 99 per cent effective, although the tubes can spontaneously reconnect, allowing for pregnancy. Tubal ligations should be considered permanent; reversals are possible but may require major surgery, and the success rates of pregnancies vary.

Are There Long-Term Effects?
Women and doctors continue to wonder whether tubal ligation adversely affects the menstrual cycle, but several studies suggest that it makes no difference to menstrual pain, the length of the cycle, or the amount of blood flow.

WHO SHOULD DO IT – HIM OR HER?

❖ Both procedures are about equally effective at preventing pregnancy. Although chance of failure is small, a failed vasectomy can be caught with follow-up semen samples; a failed

Talking about... making the sterility decision

Ron, 40, a heavy-equipment mechanic, and Martha, 39, a sign painter, have been married twenty years. They live in Wingham, Ontario. They have two children, ages 9 and 12.

Ron: The doctor said, "Well, either you're going to do it [vasectomy] or she's going to do it [tubal ligation] because we don't want her to get pregnant again." She had a few medical problems when she was pregnant.

Martha: I wasn't a good pregnant person. I had a really hard time.

Ron: And it was explained to me that it was a harder procedure for a woman to go through, a longer healing and a more serious operation. So there wasn't a great deal of choice. Why put her through it? But I was very paranoid about having a vasectomy. I was so paranoid.

Martha: I remember about the first ten times we made love after, he would say, "That's the first time it's felt normal." He said that every time. [Laughs] But for me the fear of pregnancy was gone. My sex drive has just increased ever since.

tubal ligation cannot easily be detected. A failed tubal ligation carries the risk not only of an unplanned pregnancy but of a possibly life-threatening ectopic pregnancy.

❖ Both procedures are considered to be safe. However, the need for a general anesthetic means that a tubal ligation carries more risks.

❖ Vasectomy is a simpler procedure, and in the past, an uncomplicated recovery time from vasectomy was shorter than for tubal ligation. Now, however, some doctors say the recovery time for the two is about the same.

❖ The possibility of reversal for both procedures is about the same. However, reversal of tubal ligation carries with it a risk of ectopic pregnancy.

❖ There is still some question about the link between vasectomy and prostate cancer, although most studies show no connection. There are no serious health risks associated with tubal ligation; studies conducted on links to menstrual difficulties have not shown a connection.

THE PILL AND OTHER HORMONAL OPTIONS

The birth control pill is the contraceptive of choice for most women and is now being offered to perimenopausal women to deal with symptoms of hormonal change and to prevent disease. (See Perimenopause and the Pill, page 34.) As a contraceptive, the pill was at one time considered inappropriate for women over 35 because of possible risks of heart disease. But this was later discounted and the pill is considered safe for women of all ages. However, women over 35 who smoke should not take the pill because of their already increased risk of heart disease and stroke. Although occurrences are rare, the pill is still associated with risk of blood clots, stroke, and very high blood pressure.

Today's low-dose birth control pills pack a much smaller wallop than their original sisters, which contained five times more progesterone and estrogen. Side effects, such as bloating and nausea, are also lessened. And because there are many estrogen/progesterone configurations on the market, if one causes side effects, you can try another.

Many women and their partners still don't know that emergency contraceptive (EC) pills exist for situations when other birth control fails. EC pills may prevent a pregnancy if taken within 72 hours of unprotected sex. They work by blocking fertilization or preventing a fertilized egg from being implanted in the uterine lining.

Many women and their partners still don't know that emergency contraceptive pills exist for situations when other birth control fails.

The pills are usually taken two at a time in two sessions – with the second dose following the first by twelve hours. Some women report nausea from the pills. EC pills are not 100 per cent effective; if your period does not come within three weeks, you should have a pregnancy test. To get the EC pill, you need to visit your doctor or a birth control clinic. If you use condoms, a diaphragm, spermicides, or other forms of birth control that can break or be forgotten, then you might want to have a backup EC pill package at home as insurance.

Another relatively new birth control option with particular advantages to some women over 35 is Depo-Provera, which is a progesterone hormone that is administered by injection every twelve weeks. Women who can't take the birth control pill are good candidates for Depo-Provera, which is considered safe for women who have high blood pressure, diabetes, severe migraine headaches, or tendency to blood clots, or who are over 35 and are smokers. Depo-Provera is more than 99 per cent effective. However, it does have certain side effects associated with progesterone; these include weight gain, bloating, headaches, and irregular menstrual bleeding. As well, fertility takes, on average, ten months to re-establish after the last injection.

Another long-term method that uses a synthetic progestin is called Norplant. Six small plastic rods containing the hormone are inserted into the upper arm. The rods, which slowly release hormones, can be left in place for up to five years. The side effects are similar to Depo-Provera – weight gain, headaches, and irregular bleeding. Norplant doesn't affect fertility once the rods are removed. Inserting the rods is a relatively simple process involving a small incision and a local anesthetic. Removal may take longer, and may require more than one visit.

Other Options
New barrier methods on the market for women include the contraceptive sponge, which is a small round piece of polyurethane containing spermicides. Once inserted into the vagina, it can stay in place for up to twelve hours and must be kept in place for six hours following sex. Or you can try Advantage 24, a contraceptive gel that's inserted with an applicator for twenty-four hours of protection. Then there is vcf film, which is a form of plastic wrap that is folded and inserted into the vagina at least fifteen minutes before intercourse. And, of course, there's always the diaphragm or the iud and the latex condom for him. The condom is the only form of birth control that also protects against sexually transmitted diseases.

Fertility Issues
For some couples in early midlife, the all-consuming issue is their desire to become pregnant for the first time or to have a second or third child. Dealing with the complexity of fertility problems and their treatment is beyond the scope of this book, but they must be acknowledged as a painful issue for those facing them. See the Resources for organizations that can help.

4

Food

*Sharing meals is so much a part of being a couple
that we hardly think about it, unless one of us
wants to change what's on the menu.*

If you're like most couples, you've noshed your way through your relationship. You may remember the first meal you ever had together, or the first time you cooked for the other. If you've been a couple for several years, you likely have a repertoire of meaningful meals – Friday night ordering in, Sunday family dinner, late-night snacks after sex. The contents and timing of the meals may have changed ("late night" may now be 10:30 p.m. instead of 2 a.m.), but their meaning hasn't. You have your own food language that involves whoever may be living with you – your kids, a parent – but is also just about what each of you enjoys.

Sharing meals is so much a part of being a couple that we hardly think about it, unless one of us wants to change what's on the menu. And then we both have to think a little harder – not to mention renegotiate shopping habits and cooking styles. Couples in midlife often want to change what they eat to something more healthy, less fattening, or more energizing. A diagnosis such as high blood pressure or diabetes may also make menu changes necessary. And who doesn't feel bombarded by every new study extolling the virtues of low fat, high protein, eliminating sugar, increasing fat (but just certain kinds, mind you)? In our search for health and vitality, we've become transfixed by the possibility of a magic food bullet. Surely there's a plan out there that will give us optimum health. Would it be too much to ask that it taste good too? Which brings me to Canada's Food Guide to Healthy Eating.

Would it be un-Canadian to say that I'm a little bored with the Food Guide, that sometimes I wish for a newer, jazzier approach to talking about food in this country? The Food Guide was first introduced to Canadians more than fifty years ago (I remember having to memorize it in home economics class back in Kirkland Lake the 1960s) and, in updated versions, has been the official government line on what we should eat ever since. Written in governmentese, it explains that we need to eat a variety of foods from four food groups and choose lower-fat foods more often. It seems to state the obvious. One tip for reducing fat is "Spread less butter or margarine on bread, buns, or bagels." But although familiarity may have created a wee bit of contempt, I remind myself that the advice is backed up by years of solid nutrition and food science. The Food Guide is based on Health Canada's Nutrition Recommendations – The Report of the Scientific Review Committee, which is the best scientific thinking on "the desired characteristics of the Canadian diet." That's more than can be said for the latest trendy diet being touted on daytime television.

So if the Food Guide is where we start in deciding what the two of us should be eating, what does it tell us? The first point on Canada's Guidelines for Healthy Eating is "Enjoy a VARIETY of foods." Yes, VARIETY is in capital letters so that you can't miss how important it is. And you shouldn't. It addresses several trends in modern eating habits. One is the tendency to label foods either "good" or "bad," as in "Bananas are good for you; banana splits are bad for you." In fact, no food will make or break your health. It's the overall pattern of what you eat that determines how food contributes to your health. Eating a variety of foods ensures that you get enough essential nutrients, maybe from foods you didn't even know contained them. A recent piece in *Canadian Living* about "miracle" foods pointed out that figs have lots of calcium in them and high amounts of fibre. That was news to me. As long as we eat a broad spectrum of foods, we can feel secure that we're getting the important nutrients, whether scientists have discovered all of them yet or not. Finally, to use an old cliché, variety is the spice of life. Trying new foods, new styles of cooking, and new ethnic variations makes eating a lifelong joy, which, after all, it should be.

What's a Serving?

As our daughter, Lorna, puts it, "It really bugs me trying to figure out what a serving is." In the background paper for those who teach others about the Food Guide is a warning to expect comments from the public that the Guide recommends too much food. No kidding. Even if you really like your fruits and veggies, five to ten servings a day may seem daunting until you realize that one cup of orange juice equals two servings. Because the Guide recommends serving sizes that can work for all ages and a variety of eating needs, the serving sizes start small. Once you see what one serving in each category looks like, using the Guide gets a whole lot easier. For example:

- ❖ 250 mL (1 cup) of orange juice counts as 2 servings of fruit, since 1 serving is only 125 mL (½ cup)
- ❖ 250 mL (1 cup) of broccoli counts as 2 servings of vegetables
- ❖ a whole bagel or bun, or a cup of pasta or rice, is 2 servings of grain products
- ❖ a sandwich made with 2 slices of bread counts as 2 servings of grain products.

Talking about... eating together

Patsy, 42, an office manager, and Steven, 43, a stockbroker, have been married nineteen years. They live in Mississauga, Ontario. They have two children, ages 12 and 15.

Steven: I've eaten when I really didn't want to just so Patsy wouldn't eat alone. We might stop for a snack on the way home and I'll eat even if I'm not hungry, just because I know she'll feel guilty eating by herself. I should just say "If you want to have your snack, go ahead." This reciprocal thing is just something that couples do.

Patsy: That's a very real point about reciprocal eating. If we're out for dinner and one of us has dessert, the other one feels guilty if he doesn't [keep his partner company]. And then he'll resent having had dessert.

CANADA'S FOOD GUIDE TO HEALTHY EATING

Enjoy a variety of foods from each group every day. Choose lower-fat foods more often.

	DAILY SERVINGS	
Grain products	5 to 12	Choose whole grain and enriched products more often.
Vegetables and fruit	5 to 10	Choose dark green and orange vegetables and orange fruit more often.
Milk products	Adults 2 to 4	Choose lower-fat milk products more often.
Meat and alternatives	2 to 3	Choose leaner meats, poultry, and fish, dried peas, beans and lentils more often.

Adapted from Canada's Food Guide to Healthy Eating, Health Canada, 1992. With permission of the Minister of Public Works and Government Services Canada, 1998.

Eat Together, but Don't Eat the Same as Your Spouse

Your age, body size and level of activity all affect your food needs. If you're a man between 35 and 49 who is moderately active, you need 2,700 calories from food every day on average. If you're a woman in the same age group, you need 1,900 calories or almost a third less. At 50 and over, the average man needs 2,300 calories; the average woman needs 1,800. So look at your plate of food at dinner tonight and consider whether your portions reflect your needs. Most women should be eating less than their partners, and you both should be eating considerably less than your kids. An

18-year-old boy needs 3,200 calories! Now, of course, what you have for dinner will be influenced by what each of you has eaten the rest of the day, so your dinner plates differ in other ways than just portion size. Women need more calcium, so they should have more dairy products, preferably low-fat. Before menopause, women also need more iron, so they should eat more meat and other iron-rich foods. It's ironic that men list meat – particularly steak – as their number one food craving, but it's women who may need to eat red meat more often.

Determining portion size is simple (although if you're a woman, you can sometimes feel a little deprived looking at the larger mounds of food across from you), but negotiating what will be on that dinner plate day after day can be tricky. In one couple I know, the husband is a strict vegetarian. When they moved in together, the wife gave up eating meat at home because he couldn't bear to have it in the house. She still eats meat when she goes out. That may be an extreme, but it raises the questions of who should decide what you're both eating and how you negotiate a change in your diet. In lots of couples, the chief cook and grocery shopper decides, and that's most often the woman. In more than 85 per cent of families of all ages, women say that they are the main grocery shoppers, although men shop as well. According to a food manufacturers' study, grocery shopping in one household in five is a task that's shared.

> **Most women should be eating less than their partners, and you both should be eating considerably less than your teenage kids.**

But what to eat requires much more of a negotiation than it did a generation ago. Judy Paisley, an assistant professor in the School of Nutrition at Ryerson Polytechnic University in Toronto, has studied how couples make food choices. She reports that couples told her that when they were kids, "Dad's choices determined the menu," although "Mom was responsible for kids' nutritional health." Asked who makes these decisions in their own homes, they say that they both do. Paisley says that fruit and vegetable consumption has increased in recent years partly because more women are putting these items on the menu.

COUPLE CHOICES

Your current stage in your family life cycle affects how you approach cooking. Paisley says that there are several pivotal points in a couple's gastronomic life. When you first become a couple, you create what she calls a "couple gastronomy" that defines your life apart from your families of origin. "Most people said that when they became a couple, they were open to new foods, and they changed their menus," she says. One spouse may be more adventurous than the other, which allows the less adventurous one to try new foods. "He'd try something and she'd have a taste" is how Paisley describes it.

The arrival of children changes what you've created together into a "family gastronomy." Then, once the kids move out, some couples go through an adjustment that is painful because cooking for your kids is, as Paisley says, "such an expression of parents' loving and caring for their children." But other couples seize the opportunity to be more adventurous again.

I find that not having to cook for the family means we both enjoy cooking more. Now that we don't need to be so concerned about satisfying the picky palates of our kids (Lorna is away at university and Adam, at 17, eats everything in sight), Christopher and I can explore different foods and ways of preparing them without hearing that plaintive cry "What *is* this?" Often Adam is at his part-time job over dinner and it's just the two of us. (We do make sure he eats when he gets home!) We find that we're ready to explore new

Talking about... changing food habits

Patsy, 42, an office manager, and Steven, 43, a stockbroker, have been married nineteen years. They live in Mississauga, Ontario. They have two children, ages 12 and 15.

Steven: Couples in their 40s need some sort of test to find out what part of their diet is just habit. If Patsy and I are both trying to lose weight and be a good influence on the kids, why do we have so much convenience food in the house like potato chips and soft drinks? By not having them around, we could get rid of those temptations. I know an apple would be better for me but I go for the potato chips.

Patsy: As for what food is in the house, I think that's more my judgment than his because he's hardly ever home. I'm the one dealing with temptation because I'm at home more. I try to have things that will satisfy everybody. I have a bowl of fruit on the counter and a fridge full of things like yogurt and fat-free fudgesicles. There are cookies but there are also low-fat baked potato chips. I have to satisfy the kids, too. I have a daughter who has very fussy food tastes and I can't force her to eat a piece of fruit if she doesn't want to eat a piece of fruit. So I have to have things that she will eat, too.

ideas after twenty years of asking each other which kid eats tomatoes and which one doesn't. (Trick question: they both hate them.)

FOOD AS FUEL

If you're contemplating changing what you eat, for whatever reason, realize that for both of you it's most important in midlife to
eat for energy. You can't eat as much as you did ten years ago
(unless you're prepared to change your clothing size every couple
of years), and you need to get the most out of every calorie to fuel
your busy lives.

Linda Barton, a consulting dietitian in Kitchener, Ontario,
counsels many couples who are changing their food habits.
"They can help one another – or not," she says. She gives the
example of a couple watching TV together. He's eating peanuts
but she isn't because they both agree that peanuts are too fattening
for her. So when he goes out of the room during a commercial,
she grabs handfuls, and then feels major guilt. Barton says that
when these partners explore their attitudes in such a scenario,
they decide to change the snack to one they can both share.

People who make poor food choices and then express guilt –
"We shouldn't be doing it" – are really saying that they are bored
or exhausted or just way too busy, Barton says. Couples may
come home at the end of the week with the idea that "it's Friday
night, so it's party night." As a result, they eat too much, too late,
and wake up with a food hangover on Saturday morning. Barton
asks them to re-examine their choices. "I say, 'Tell me the feeling
you want to get and we'll work toward that feeling.'" If they say
that what they want to do is relax and feel good together, she asks,
"How are the chips helping?" Rethinking their Friday night routine to include a healthy snack when they walk through the door,
then a half-hour time-out to have a hot bath or go for a walk, can
achieve the good feelings they're after, she says.

Eat for Energy

Consulting dietitian Linda Barton says timing is everything when it comes to eating for energy. For maximum performance, you should eat every three or four hours. Don't shy away from between-meal snacks. They're essential. Barton has a unique approach to planning meals and snacks. She calls it the 1-2-3 energy package. Using Canada's Food Guide to Healthy Eating, make up each meal or snack to include one of each of the following:

1. A vegetable or fruit, which will give you a carbohydrate energy boost lasting about one hour.

2. A grain, which provides longer-lasting carbohydrate energy, about two hours.

3. A protein, which provides energy for about three hours.

The BIG Midlife Eating Issue

OK, LET'S DEAL WITH FAT

First of all, too much dietary fat is bad for you. All dietary fat – saturated or unsaturated – has more of the calories that make *you* fat. Saturated fat promotes the production of the "bad" cholesterol, which, in turn, can cause heart disease and kidney failure and is linked to cancer. Before this fat saga goes any further, you need details on the cast of characters. You will be forgiven if you've forgotten who's who.

Saturated fat – This is a "bad guy." Saturated fats are found most-ly in animal products – meat and dairy foods. They trigger the liver to produce "bad" low-density lipoprotein (LDL) cholesterol in the blood, which sticks to the walls of your arteries. Narrowed arteries impede the flow of blood, a condition known as athero-sclerosis. Atherosclerosis can cause high blood pressure because the heart must pump harder to push the same volume of blood through the narrowed arteries. Narrowed coronary arteries – the arteries leading to the heart – can cause coronary artery disease and lead to heart attack. Narrowed arteries to the kidneys can cause kidney failure.

Trans fats – A recently introduced "bad guy." Trans fats are the result of hydrogenation, the manufacturing process that turns liquid fats into solids. They can be found in vegetable shortening or hydrogenated vegetable oil and all foods containing these ingredients, like cookies, crackers, other baked goods, and con-venience products. They have the same effect on blood choles-terol as saturated fats.

Unsaturated fats – Definitely a "good guy" – or should that be "good guys"? Unsaturated fats come from vegetables and some fish. There are two kinds of unsaturated fats – monounsaturated (olive, avocado, and peanut oils) and polyunsaturated (which includes fish and most other vegetable oils, such as corn oil). Unsaturated fats stimulate the production of "good" high-densi-ty lipoprotein (HDL) cholesterol in the liver. HDL cholesterol actually clears the clogging LDL cholesterol out of arteries and therefore reduces the risk of atherosclerosis.

To keep these fats straight in your mind, remember that saturated fats are usually solid at room temperature, whereas unsaturated fats are usually liquid. Trans fats are more difficult to track because they're found in processed food. You have to become a label sleuth. Look for these words – *hydrogenated* or *partially hydrogenated* – in the list of ingredients. Health Canada plans to release new labelling guidelines that require food manufacturers to identify how much trans fat is in their products.

Most of us eat too much fat of all kinds. Fat should constitute no more than 30 per cent of your daily food intake. A man should eat no more than 90 grams of fat a day from all sources, and a woman no more than 65 grams. I don't suggest that you start counting grams by the mouthful, but these two numbers – commit them to memory – give you a benchmark when you're checking a label or a recipe for fat content. When looking recently for a dessert recipe, I found one that sounded good. Then I checked the fat content – 27 grams of fat per serving. One serving would provide more than a third of each person's fat intake for the day. None of us could afford that, so I kept looking.

Don't worry too much about the numbers (although for you math whizzes I will keep including a few of them). Instead, look at what you eat and figure out where the bulk of your fat comes from. Forty per cent of the fat in Canadians' diets comes from what the Food Guide calls "other foods." This includes food that is just about all fat – margarine, butter, vegetable oil, regular mayonnaise, some salad dressing. Cookbook author Anne Lindsay, who is also *Canadian Living*'s nutrition editor, says that when people tell her that they've changed their cooking because of her advice, most say that they are using more herbs and spices instead of fat to add flavour to their food. Adding fresh gingerroot or doubling the cinnamon in a recipe creates great tastes and people don't miss the fat. "People are really amazed that they enjoy their food just as much or even more," she says.

"Other foods" also include really high-fat snack foods like potato chips, corn chips, and cheesies. And here for many people, the main culprit is the on-the-run snack. You don't have time for lunch and end up eating a bag of potato chips in the car on the way to an appointment. Or you both get home from work famished and before you know it, you've gone through a round of Brie cheese on crackers before the pasta water's even boiling. Solution: Plan your snacks. Keep a bag of popcorn (without the butter!) in your drawer at work for that car ride. (Yes, it would be better to have lunch, but plan for your lapses.) Keep a bag of baby carrots and yogurt dip in the fridge to tide you over until dinner is ready.

Anne Lindsay says that reducing fat in your diet is a gradual process. "Most people don't make huge, dramatic changes. They might start by switching from 2 per cent to 1 per cent milk; then they put part-skim mozzarella on their pizza. They might fry foods less often. Gradually, they choose lower-fat products. That's what most people do." And that's what the two of you can do, too.

When Anne does seminars on healthy cooking with lower-fat ingredients, she uses these charts from two of her cookbooks to highlight where fat may be hidden – check out the grams of fat in mayo and olive oil!

USE LEANER SPREADS ON YOUR BREAD

1 TBSP (15 mL)	CALORIES	FAT (g)	PROTEIN (g)
1% b.f. cottage cheese	12	trace	2
skim-milk processed cheese spread	30	1	4
light cream cheese	36	3	1
Processed Cheddar cheese spread	46	3	3
cream cheese	51	5	1
jelly or jam	54	0	0
peanut butter	93	8	4
butter or margarine	101	11	trace

Lindsay, Anne. *Anne Lindsay's Light Kitchen*. 1994. Macmillan Canada. Reprinted with permission.

COMPARE SALAD DRESSING INGREDIENTS

1 TBSP (15 ML)	FAT (g)	SATURATED FAT (g)	CALORIES
Oil – canola, olive, sunflower, corn, safflower	14	1-2	120
Mayonnaise	11	1	100
Light mayonnaise	5	0.4	50
Miracle Whip	7	0.4	69
Miracle Whip Light	4	0.2	43
Sour cream (14% b.f.)	3	2	28
Light sour cream	2	1.3	23
Cottage cheese (2% b.f.)	0.3	0.2	13
Yogurt (1.5% b.f.)	0.2	0.2	10
Buttermilk	0.1	Trace	6

Lindsay, Anne. *Lighthearted Everyday Cooking.* 1991. Macmillan of Canada. Reprinted with permission.

You Know Diets Don't Work, So How Come One-Third of Us Are Dieting?

I felt like skipping this section because I feel as if I've read every-thing I've ever wanted on dieting and its perils, and I thought you probably have, too. But the fact is that one-third of us are dieting. More women than men diet although more men than women are overweight. As a culture, we are obsessed with weight loss, but it is a special preoccupation in midlife because between the ages of 25 and 55 the average weight gain is about twenty pounds. As I sifted through the research, I decided that even though more women than men are dieting, we women are much more cynical about the whole business. Ever since we picked up our first teen magazine, we've been bombarded by dieting information – dos and don'ts, perils, promises. The bombardment never stops. When I turned on my computer this morning, I had a junk e-mail message from SkinnyGal. Subject: "Eat! Sleep! And still lose weight! No joke!" I hit delete. So for the men who haven't read a dieting article a month since they were 13, here's a summary of the latest thinking on the problem with dieting.

How Do We Diet?	This Is What Really Happens
by skipping meals or decreasing calories	❖ Our brains go into starvation mode and this lowers our metabolism so that our bodies store fat more easily from fewer calories. ❖ The demand for fuel from our brains and muscles causes "rebound munchies," usually for high-fat and high-sugar foods. ❖ We experience the results of energy deprivation and poor attention span, irritability, and fatigue. ❖ We may lose muscle mass.
by cutting out the carbohydrates from starchy foods	❖ Our body loses its best source of stable energy, so we are more likely to feel moody and tired. ❖ We end up eating high-fat and sugary foods to satisfy "munchies."
by cutting out the proteins from meats	❖ We may not get enough iron, which leads to fatigue. ❖ The energy we do get from meals may not last as long, which causes more hunger between meals.
by going on preplanned meal replacement diet or liquid diet	❖ We have a 95 per cent chance of regaining within one or two years any weight we lose. ❖ We give control of the diet to the plan, which lowers our self-esteem. ❖ We lose muscle mass along with fat, which lowers our metabolism, making it even more likely that our body will store fat on fewer calories. ❖ Our habits are replaced temporarily, not changed permanently. ❖ These diet programs can be very expensive.
by fasting	❖ Most of the weight loss is water. ❖ Muscle mass decreases, which lowers metabolism, resulting in subsequent weight gain. ❖ Fasting can be dangerous for some individuals.

Source: B.C. Ministry of Health and Ministry Responsible for Seniors

But the fact that diets don't work doesn't help with our weight loss issue. One-third of North Americans are obese, and some scientists claim that obesity has now become a leading cause of illness and early death in the Western world, second only to tobacco smoking. How did we reach this?

The factors that contribute to obesity include our genetic makeup, physiological changes, and psychological influences. But at its most simple, we're getting fatter because we're eating more calories in food than we're expending in physical activity.

Over the decades of the twentieth century, technological advances in transportation, electrical appliances, and tools for home and work transformed daily life. The car, the computer, and the weed whacker have reduced the amount of physical activity people must do to survive. Levels of affluence vary, but most people have access to a wide selection of foods, including high-fat, high-sugar (therefore high-calorie) processed (there's that technology again) foods, and we eat more of everything, from steaks to pasta to Twinkies.

While our technological wizardry has unfortunately made us fatter, we humans have created a culture of thinness that we celebrate in our supermodels and our pop stars. Perverse as we are, as our real bodies have become fatter, our idealized images of appealing bodies have become thinner. No wonder we go crazy over diets.

It takes a strong man or woman to withstand the multiple pressures of food advertising, media hype about the sexiness of thin, and the latest news story about the obesity epidemic. But these are pressures best withstood when you're middle-aged and married. What should you do? The first step is to figure out whether your weight worries are a health problem, an appearance problem, or no problem at all for either of you.

UNHEALTHY FLAB

Remember, men get most of their health information from their spouses, so women readers might want to share the Body Mass Index (BMI) chart (see page 123) and waist-to-hip-ratio formula (see below) with their partners, who may never have come across either before. (I know that most women have fiddled with these numbers on occasion.) The Body Mass Index is derived from the measure of your weight in kilograms divided by your height in metres squared. Check your numbers on the BMI chart (see page 123). If your BMI is over 27, you're considered obese, which means that you face a fourfold increase in your risk of diabetes, stroke, and heart attack. A BMI between 25 and 27 means that your health may be at risk because of your weight. Take it as a warning sign that you don't have much leeway.

Another measure of obesity is the waist-to-hip ratio, which measures how your fat is distributed on your body. Fat over the abdomen (which gives you an "apple" shape) with a ratio of waist to hip greater than .9 for women and 1.0 for men, is most likely a health risk. To figure out your ratio, measure around your waist and your hips, then divide your waist measure by your hip measure.

Avoid Pills

Be very cautious about trying an appetite suppressant. Your doctor should prescribe it for only a few weeks and only in conjunction with counselling and a plan for increased physical activity. In one of the more spectacular pharmacological failings related to weight loss, the combination of two drugs, fenfluramine and phentermine resin – known as fen-phen – produced good weight loss results, but at a price. About a third of the patients taking the combination suffered heart valve abnormalities. Fenfluramine was taken off the U.S. and Canadian markets in 1997.

If these numbers reveal that one of you has a weight or fat problem, then deal with it as a health issue. Get some expert help from your family doctor or a dietitian.

Both of you probably need to revamp your eating and physical activity habits to bring your bodies slowly back into balance. It probably took you twenty years to get out of balance (if you were ever in balance). It may take a year or two to get back into balance. Midlife, a time of being in control and less susceptible to outside pressures, is a perfect time to make these adjustments.

IT's "ONLY"APPEARANCE

If your BMI and waist-to-hip ratio reveal that you're not facing a health issue but rather an appearance issue, you have two choices. You can choose to love your body (and your partner's body) with love handles and a little extra padding or you can fine-tune your eating patterns and physical activity levels to take off the few kilograms that are irritating you. Again, expect to take several months to undo several years of imbalance. But keep your expectations realistic. Our metabolism slows as we age. Small weight gains during midlife – a pound a year – are to be expected and may even be beneficial, particularly for women. Because estrogen is stored in fat tissue, women with more fat tissue may have fewer symptoms of menopause than women who are thin.

And what if, in spite of good advice, one of you is determined to try a new diet you heard about at the office? The diet you're most likely to try is the "high-protein, low-carbohydrate" diet that's been gaining momentum since biochemist Barry Sears first published *Enter The Zone* (HarperCollins) back in 1995. In the short term, you'll lose weight, but the diet is difficult to follow and it's likely that you'll regain the weight quickly. There are risks of stress to your kidneys. At least take the precautions listed by dietitian Denise Beatty in a piece in *Canadian Living*:

Body Mass Index

Height	19	20	21	22	23	24	25	26	27	28	29	30	35	40
							Weight							
4'10"	91	96	100	105	110	115	119	124	129	134	138	143	167	191
4'11"	94	99	104	109	114	119	124	128	133	138	143	148	173	198
5'0"	97	102	107	112	118	123	128	133	138	143	148	153	179	204
5'1"	100	106	111	116	122	127	132	137	143	148	153	158	185	211
5'2"	104	109	115	120	126	131	136	142	147	153	158	163	191	218
5'3"	107	113	118	124	130	135	141	146	152	158	163	169	197	225
5'4"	110	116	122	128	134	140	145	151	157	163	169	174	204	232
5'5"	114	120	126	132	138	144	150	156	162	168	174	180	210	240
5'6"	118	124	130	136	142	148	155	161	167	173	180	186	216	247
5'7"	121	127	134	140	146	153	159	166	172	178	185	191	223	255
5'8"	125	131	138	144	151	158	164	171	177	184	190	197	230	262
5'9"	128	135	142	149	155	162	169	176	182	189	196	203	236	270
5'10"	132	139	146	153	160	167	174	181	188	195	202	209	243	278
5'11"	136	143	150	157	165	172	179	186	193	200	208	215	250	286
6'0"	140	147	154	162	169	177	184	191	199	206	213	221	258	294
6'1"	144	151	159	166	174	182	189	197	204	212	219	227	265	302
6'2"	148	155	163	171	179	186	194	202	210	218	225	233	272	311
6'3"	152	160	168	176	184	192	200	208	216	224	232	240	279	319
6'4"	156	164	172	180	189	197	205	213	221	230	238	246	287	328

Lower than 20
Health risks include high blood pressure, depression, and anemia

20 to 25
Your weight is not likely to be associated with health problems

26 to 27
Caution zone – could lead to health problems for some

Higher than 27
Increasing risk of health problems, including high blood pressure, diabetes, certain cancers, arthritis, poor mental health

❖ Discuss the diet with your doctor, particularly if you have heart problems, liver or kidney disease, lupus, or if you use steroid or diuretic medications.

❖ Consider the diet only for a short-term jump-start (say, two weeks) to weight loss. Plan for a gradual transition to a healthier, more balanced eating plan.

❖ Begin a daily exercise program (start with walking).

❖ Be sure to drink eight to ten glasses of water a day (or the equivalent).

❖ Be alert for danger signs: extreme fatigue, dizziness or light-headedness, dehydration, heart palpitations, difficulty urinating.

Eating to Beat Disease

One of the markers of midlife, to be callous about it, is a greater awareness of your probable life span or how much time you may have left. And your family history gives you the clue. What risks of cancer, heart disease, osteoporosis, diabetes do you each face? If you decide to customize your diet to minimize those risks, you'll find that Canada's Food Guide to Healthy Eating has beat you to it. The guide has been designed in collaboration with such organizations as the Heart and Stroke Foundation and the Canadian Cancer Society. Here's what to focus on to reduce risk.

TO REDUCE THE RISK OF CANCER

❖ Boost your intake of fruits and vegetables. A review by the World Cancer Research Fund and the American Institute for Cancer Research of more than 4,500 studies found that fruits and vegetables were the common denominator in protection against many kinds of cancers. It may be the antioxidants (vitamins E, C, A and beta-carotene) found in fruits and vegetables as well as grain products that offer the protection. Other nutrients are also important. A recent study of almost 50,000 male health professionals linked lycopene found in tomatoes with reduced incidence of prostate cancer.

- Reduce fat intake.
- Limit alcohol intake.
- Avoid salt-preserved, nitrate-preserved, and smoked foods.
- Eat food that has been barbecued, charred, or roasted only occasionally. The deep brown surface that comes from cooking at high heat contains polycyclic aromatic hydrocarbons, which can cause cancer.

TO REDUCE THE RISK OF OSTEOPOROSIS

- Boost your calcium intake. Drink milk and eat hard cheese and yogurt, broccoli, collards, kale, bok choy, and the soft bones in canned salmon and sardines.
- Reduce calcium loss. Avoid excess salt, excess caffeine, and excess protein, all of which can strip calcium from your body.
- Get adequate amounts of vitamin D. The simplest way to get enough vitamin D is to get out in the sunshine. But in Canada from November to March, there isn't enough sunshine. If you drink milk, you'll get enough vitamin D from it; otherwise consider a supplement.

TO REDUCE THE RISK OF HEART DISEASE

- Cut your fat intake to reduce your blood cholesterol level. Eat more fruits and vegetables, grains and cereals, and smaller

Talking about... diet and disease

John, 50, and Simone, 49, are partners in a boat manufacturing business. They live in Halifax, Nova Scotia. They've been married for twenty-eight years. John was diagnosed with Type II diabetes about twenty years ago. Simone had a minor heart attack (with no residual damage) about three years ago and has recently been diagnosed with osteoporosis. They have two adult daughters.

John: The diet for diabetics has changed dramatically over twenty years. Before, you measured food on little scales, but now the magic word is *exercise*. And you can have the odd bit of pizza or ice cream; it doesn't pose a major danger if you don't overdo it. But it's a matter of adjusting my lifestyle, which has been a tough challenge for me. I miss junk food. I went through all the diabetes clinics, but I didn't work very hard at applying them to myself. Simone did more of that for me.

Simone: I am totally responsible for his diet. He makes me responsible, and I accept that. The way we changed our diet when John was diagnosed with diabetes was to eat more fresh fruit and vegetables. He's not big on veggies so I have to disguise them. I make a lot of soups and purée the vegetables. For me [with osteoporosis], I just made a choice that we'd eat more high-calcium foods. Occasionally, we both get cravings for a really good ice cream. And occasionally we have it. We allow for that excess.

John: To give more credit to what Simone has done, she's had her own osteoporosis to deal with and my diabetes to deal with. We have one daughter who went through a huge vegetarian stage. And our second daughter is lactose-intolerant.

Simone: We've had very interesting lifestyles here. Some Christmases, we've had a nut loaf and a turkey.

portions of meats and other sources of saturated fats. Focus on reducing trans fats in your diet by eating fewer baked goods and convenience foods.

❖ Eat fish two or three times a week. Fish, particularly fattier fish, like salmon and mackerel, contains omega-3 fatty acids, a type of polyunsaturated fat that lowers blood triglycerides.

❖ Reduce your sodium intake. Canadians consume about twenty times the amount of salt we need. Most people just excrete the extra salt in their urine. But "sodium-sensitive" people can't. If you are sodium-sensitive, a high salt intake may predispose you to hypertension, which leads to strokes, heart attacks, and other illnesses. About half of all people with hypertension are sodium-sensitive. Many canned, processed, snack, and fast foods have high levels of salt. So do cheese and many dry cereals.

❖ Get enough vitamin B_6, B_{12}, and folic acid to reduce high homocysteine levels, which are linked to heart attacks. For B_{12}, eat liver, eggs, milk and milk products, and seafood; for B_6 eat liver, fish (particularly herring and salmon), brown rice, and bananas; for folic acid, eat broccoli, peas, romaine lettuce, and lentils.

❖ Double up on soluble fibre. This form of fibre is helpful in controlling blood sugar and lowering blood cholesterol. The best sources of soluble fibre are oat bran, oatmeal, legumes (including dried beans, peas, and lentils), pectin-rich fruit (including apples, strawberries, and citrus fruit), and psyllium.

TO REDUCE THE RISK OF DIABETES

❖ No food or food group has been shown to reduce the risk of diabetes, but food is still a factor. The best advice for reducing your risk of diabetes is to control your weight.

Soy – In a Class by Itself

Soy has been touted as the way to reduce the risks and symptoms of several health conditions. Studies link the plant estrogens in soy to a decrease in menopausal symptoms, such as hot flashes. They are also linked to lower cholesterol levels, stronger bones, and a lower risk of breast and prostate cancer. Although none of these connections has been proved beyond doubt, there's enough evidence to suggest that both of you should include soy as part of your diet. But finding ways to include soy in your meals takes some experimenting. More and more soy products are flooding into the grocery stores, so toss one of the new ones into your grocery cart periodically. Try soy milk on your cereal or in a fruit shake. Go out to a Japanese restaurant and order a bean curd dish. From *Anne Lindsay's New Light Cooking* (Ballantine Books, 1998), here are some suggestions for getting your soy:

❖ Add tofu or tempeh (a fermented, chewy soybean product that can be used as a meat replacement) to soups, stews, stir-fries, and salads.

❖ Use tofu or textured vegetable protein in place of cheese and meat in casseroles, chili, tacos, and spaghetti sauce.

❖ Mix soy flour with other flours to make muffins or pancakes.

❖ Use some soy milk in dishes when cooking or baking.

Supplements

If bottles of supplements are accumulating in your cupboard, you're part of the big experiment. Half of us are popping vitamin pills regularly to prevent illnesses, to balance out an unbalanced diet, and to boost energy. One of the researchers on this book, Susan Pedwell, wrote in a piece for *Canadian Living* that "if you buy vitamins as a fast fix for a haphazard diet, you may be further ahead if you spend your money on, say, a box of raspberries." Unlike vitamin pills, real food contains fibre, complex carbohydrates, and a host of compounds whose benefits scientists are just starting to understand. And you get to eat the real food.

Eating even the minimum number of servings of each of the four food groups in Canada's Food Guide to Healthy Eating will give you all the nutrients you need to prevent deficiencies. However, there are some people who could benefit from supplementary vitamins:

Unlike vitamin pills, real food contains fibre, complex carbohydrates, and a host of compounds whose benefits scientists are just starting to understand.

❖ pregnant women
❖ dieters who consume less than 1,800 calories a day
❖ heavy drinkers who replace food with alcohol
❖ seniors who don't have much appetite or who have problems chewing and swallowing
❖ people with food allergies or sensitivities to commonly used foods (wheat, other grains, milk products, eggs, nuts, soy products).

Many of us take vitamins not just to prevent deficiencies but to reap potential extra health benefits, such as protection from heart disease or cancer. Although much is still unknown about the benefits and risks of the vitamins readily available in drugstores and health food stores, here are five supplements to consider. (When buying vitamins, look for a drug identification number [DIN]; it signals that the pill is sold as a drug not a food, which means that it must meet set standards.)

Multivitamin – This is the most commonly used supplement and is taken as insurance against an inadequate diet. Women who are menstruating may benefit from the iron content to offset any iron deficiency from blood loss.

Precautions: Don't double up – you might exceed safe limits for some nutrients.

Calcium – You both need adequate amounts of calcium to slow down bone loss. Although recommendations are in flux, the Osteoporosis Society of Canada says that adults aged 19 to 49 need 1,000 mg a day from food and supplements; those over 49 need 1,000 to 1,500 mg a day. One cup (8 oz) of milk gives you 315 mg. Orange juice with calcium added is now available. If you aren't getting enough calcium from your diet, consider using a calcium supplement. Include a vitamin D tablet because it aids calcium absorption, but don't exceed 400 IU per day.

Precautions: Some calcium preparations contain lead. Avoid also those made from dolomite, bone meal, or oyster shell.

Vitamin E – Although studies are still inconclusive, vitamin E may reduce risk of heart disease, cataracts, and some cancers; it may slow the aging process. Its effectiveness in preventing disease is linked to dosages of at least 100 IU a day (from both food and supplements); 300 IU a day is considered safe.

Precautions: High dosages of vitamin E may increase the risk of bleeding and stroke if taken with an anticoagulant such as aspirin or warfarin (Coumadin or Warfilone). High doses may also increase risk of bleeding during surgery and reduce the absorption of vitamins A, D, and K.

Folic Acid – Supplements of folic acid may reduce the risk of having a baby with spina bifida or neural tube defects by 50 to 70 per cent. Since half of all pregnancies are unplanned, some rec-

ommend that all women of child-bearing age take a daily supplement of 0.4 mg of folic acid. This amount is usually contained in
a multivitamin. Folic acid, along with vitamins B_6 and B_{12}, can
also reduce the level of homocysteine, which has been linked to
cardiovascular disease. (See Folic Acid, page 258.)

Precaution: Don't exceed 1 mg of folic acid daily.

5

Sleep

*Your chance of getting a good night's sleep
often depends on your partner.*

Curling up together to sleep at the end of the day can be one of the simple pleasures of being a couple. It can also be a major irritation – when one of you is punching the pillow just as the other is about to drift off, or when one or both of you snore. Your chance of getting a good night's sleep often depends on your partner. However, several of the physical and lifestyle changes of midlife can make that good sleep more elusive, if no less necessary, for both of you.

His Sleep, Her Sleep

As we age, our need for sleep doesn't change much, but the quality of our sleep does. Dr. J. Paul Caldwell, in his book *Sleep* (Key Porter Books, 1995), says, "Sleep simply gets worse." Cheerful thought. The amount of deep sleep decreases gradually in both sexes until a 40-year-old gets only about half as much deep sleep as a 20-year-old. This may explain why we find it so infuriating that our teenage children manage to sleep through anything and everything. We should be so lucky.

If either of you works shifts, you may find it harder to handle the shift changes, especially after the age of 50, Caldwell says. Shift changes affect the amount of deep sleep you get, which is already at a premium. If you have a choice, this is the time to move to permanent days. But if you must work shifts, try to work the same shift on a regular basis, rather than rotate shifts. Your body can adapt to this more readily than if you have to readjust your schedule for each shift change.

A Primer on Sleep

Evidence grows that sleep is crucial to your health, particularly in protecting your immune system. In his book *Sleep Thieves* (Simon & Schuster, 1997), Vancouver psychologist Stanley Coren describes the nasty deaths of laboratory rats who were felled by infectious microorganisms that seem to have penetrated their immune systems because they were sleep deprived. Most of us don't need rat experiments to know that when we don't get enough sleep, we're more susceptible to whatever bug is going around, or that if we do get sick, we improve faster when we listen to our bodies telling us to get extra sleep.

Letting our bodies dictate the amount of sleep we need is not something we do very well anymore, although we shouldn't blame ourselves too much. It's easy – even expected – in our culture of 24-hour assembly lines and all-night drugstores to view sleep as an unnecessary interruption. Over the last century, the amount of sleep people in general get has changed, as have our attitudes to sleep. Before the electric light bulb blurred the activities of day and night, adults spent 1½ hours more a night sleeping than do adults today.

Lack of sleep makes you feel irritable and less able to cope with day-to-day activities because your short-term memory is impaired. Your mood is lower and you're not much fun to live with. If you continue getting less sleep than you need, over time you accumulate a sleep debt. If you need eight hours of sleep every night, but for a week you get only seven hours, by the end of the week, you're seven hours in debt. That sleep debt of seven hours will make you sleepy during the day, more moody, less quick in your reaction times.

Just what is a good night's sleep? Most adults need about eight hours sleep, although some of us need less and some need more. Coren maintains that most of us function best after ten hours sleep but that we can get by with eight. When we get less than ten, we reduce our "cushion" for those times when something disrupts our sleep. In other words, we fall into sleep debt fast, he says.

A good night's sleep actually includes two kinds of sleep – rapid eye movement (REM) and non-rapid eye movement (NREM). During NREM, body functions such as heart rate and brain functioning gradually slow down in stages until you reach the deepest, most restful sleep, called slow wave, or deep, sleep. During REM sleep, body functions and dreaming increase. In the course of the night, you move between the two phases of sleep. Research suggests that slow wave NREM sleep may restore us physically while REM sleep may affect intellect and memory.

Women report more sleep problems than men. For many women, sleep or the lack of it is a motherhood issue. Whether they're listening for a baby's cry or a teen's key in the lock, women are more attuned to the nighttime needs of their kids.

HORMONES AND ZZZZ'S

We're just starting to know more about how female reproductive hormones affect women's sleep. For a long time, women were excluded from sleep studies because of their menstrual cycles. As it turns out, hormone cycles bring some predictable changes to sleep.

Menstrual cycle – The week or so before a woman's period, she may waken more often during the night and experience less deep sleep. After her period, when her estrogen levels are rising, she may experience her best sleep of the cycle. But these changes are individual, and not every woman will notice them. Women with other symptoms of premenstrual syndrome, such as weight gain and mood changes, are more likely to notice sleep problems with their cycles.

Pregnancy – Being very sleepy is a common complaint of early pregnancy, probably due to hormonal changes. And sleep becomes elusive in late pregnancy because of discomfort.

Menopause – For many women, menopause wreaks havoc with sleep because of hot flashes. In fact, some of the complaints women attribute to menopause – insomnia, daytime fatigue, moodiness – may be caused by interruptions in their sleep. Even if a night sweat or a hot flash doesn't actually wake you up, it can interfere with sleep enough to affect how you feel the next day. Alleviating the hot flashes improves your sleep. (See The Hot Flash, page 35.)

HIS AND HER SLEEP HABITS

Your sleep routine is one health habit that is improved by living with a partner. However, your sleep habits (what the experts call "sleep hygiene") take on new meaning in midlife as you become attuned to each other's changes in sleep patterns. Many couples say they sleep better together than apart. And sleep research shows that couples accommodate each other in bed. Couples photographed in sleep labs perform a night-long tango. When one rolls over, the other usually rolls in the same direction.

Reduce the touching of your bodies to minimize sleep disturbances. In *Sleep*, Paul Caldwell says that too many couples sleep in beds that are too small. If one of you wakes up every time the other turns over, you may need a bigger bed, or even two beds pushed together. And if your partner works shifts, snores loudly, or has a very different circadian rhythm – one of you is a night owl and the other is an early bird – then separate beds may make more sense for you. Don't look at separate beds as a sign that you've given up on your sex life. Just think of the other's bed as another choice of location for lovemaking.

Along with investing in a nice big bed, there are simple habits you can both follow to help ensure good sleep.

During the day, stick to a routine:

* Even if your bedtime fluctuates, get up at the same time every morning. Eventually your body will get the message to be tired at the appropriate time in the evening.
* Exercise the same amount and at the same time each day. Avoid vigorous exercise in the evening, although an evening stroll might be helpful.
* Avoid napping during the day. (If you don't have trouble sleeping, then napping can be beneficial. See What About Naps?, page 140.)
* Eat your meals at regular times, and don't eat a heavy or spicy meal in the evening. Don't drink large amounts of liquids in the evening.

In the evening, let your body relax:

* Eliminate caffeine in the evenings and reduce your total daily intake if you think caffeine affects your sleep.
* Eliminate nicotine as a stimulant in your body. Quit smoking or, at least, don't smoke cigarettes in the evening.

❖ Give yourself time to wind down before going to bed. Have a warm bath or a light snack.

❖ Don't use alcohol as a sedative. It will make you sleepy, but your sleep will be fragmented. Using alcohol as a sedative might develop into a problem.

❖ Make your bedroom comfortable, quiet, and dark. Mask any disturbing noises with more soothing background noise such as from a fan. Keep the bedroom temperature around 18°C (65°F).

❖ Go to bed when you're sleepy and not before.

Once you're in bed:

❖ Don't discuss problems, don't argue, don't rehash the day's events. Instead of bringing your worries to bed, write them out to be dealt with the next day.

❖ Revisit happy memories or events in your mind.

❖ Have sex. An orgasm has a sedative effect.

❖ Don't watch the clock. Turn the face away from you so that it is out of sight.

❖ If you haven't fallen asleep within half an hour, don't stay in bed. Get up and do something relaxing such as reading or watching TV until you feel sleepy.

❖ Sleep as long as you need to feel good the next day, and don't stay in bed any longer than you need to. Too much time in bed can make your sleep shallow.

WHAT ABOUT NAPS?

From the time we were first married, my husband, Christopher, has always loved his catnaps and would shut his eyes for fifteen or twenty minutes for a rejuvenating boost after a tough day or to make up for a late night. That's if I would let him. A nap, as far as I was concerned, wasn't good for your nighttime sleep. And besides, there was something a little unseemly about sleeping in the middle of the day, wasn't there? Then I, too, discovered the power of the nap and became a convert. Scientists now tell us that napping can help boost our performance and help us function better. The optimum length for a nap varies from individual to individual, but even naps as short as ten minutes can have a restorative effect. While most of us wouldn't think of having a nap at work, that's the place where we would probably get the most benefit. A well-timed nap can boost productivity, enhance safety, and help relieve the fatigue caused by rotating shifts.

Insomnia

Most of us have occasional nights when we can't sleep because we're stressed out about something at work or we had an argument over who was supposed to have paid the hydro bill. That's not insomnia, that's just having a bad night. Insomnia, which afflicts 30 to 35 per cent of Canadians, is an ongoing problem of too little sleep that affects day-to-day functioning. You're less alert, your memory and concentration aren't as good, and your mood may be low. Insomnia can be the result of not being able to fall asleep, waking up often in the night, or waking early in the morning. Sleep experts classify insomnia by how long it lasts and what causes it.

Transient – a few nights of poor sleep, perhaps caused by jet lag.

Short-term – up to three weeks, usually caused by stress, such as losing your job or a family illness.

Long-term – more than three weeks and may be caused by an underlying problem such as depression.

More women than men suffer from insomnia, and the gap widens with age. Not surprisingly, the lower your income, the more likely you are to have insomnia. Lack of funds is a major stress that can affect your sleep. Nor is it a surprise that couch potatoes are more likely to be insomniacs than people who are physically active.

SLEEP DIFFICULTIES BY AGE

Age	Men	Women
25 to 44	19 per cent	23 per cent
45 to 64	19 per cent	32 per cent

SLEEP DIFFICULTIES BY INCOME

Lowest	47 per cent
Lower middle	32 per cent
Middle	25 per cent
Upper middle	21 per cent
Highest	18 per cent

Source: Statistics Canada General Social Survey 1991

CAFFEINE-INDUCED INSOMNIA

Caffeine is the drug of choice for 80 per cent of adults. But the daily jolt can have a negative effect on sleep patterns and increase the number of times you awaken in the night. Most of us get our hit from coffee. But coffee isn't the only source. Some medications contain caffeine. Here's the caffeine content of some common beverages, according to the Canadian Pharmacists Association.

PRODUCT	CAFFEINE (mg)
Coffees (per 150 mL)	
Percolated	75–140
Instant	60–90
Decaffeinated	2–6
Filter drip	110–280
Teas (per 150 mL)	
Herbal	25–140
Regular	45–110
Iced	30–80
Soft Drinks/Colas (per 350 mL)	
Coca-Cola	33
Ginger Ale	0
Mountain Dew	54
Pepsi-Cola	38
7Up	0
Tab	32
Cocoa Drinks	
Hot cocoa (240 mL)	50
Chocolate milk (225 mL)	27

Reprinted with permission from *Nonprescription Drug Reference for Health Professionals*, page 591. Published by the Canadian Pharmacists Association, Ottawa © 1996.

GETTING TREATMENT

Although most people who suffer from insomnia don't even bother to mention it to their doctors (and doctors sometimes don't ask), it's a serious problem that affects just about every aspect of the sufferer's life and deserves treatment. About two-thirds of chronic insomniacs have some other condition that may also need treatment. For example, the insomniacs who suffer from depression or anxiety may respond to treatment with an anti-depressant. However, some anti-depressants, such as selective serotonin reuptake inhibitors, can actually disrupt sleep. Conditions such as sleep apnea or restless leg syndrome can be treated and sleep is restored. But about one-third of people suffering from long-term insomnia don't have any identifiable underlying cause.

Whatever the cause of your insomnia, you need to talk to your family physician about it. Take your partner along to the appointment. In fact, he or she may beg to go and get to the bottom of this. Your partner may have a more accurate take on your snoring or sleep apnea than you do. You may want to keep a daily sleep diary together that includes bedtimes, how long it takes you to fall asleep, the number of times you wake in the night, and the total amount of sleep each of you gets each night. Other information to include: daytime naps, exercise routine, use of caffeine, drugs, and alcohol.

Your treatment should include counselling to help you change your behaviour and improve your sleep habits. It may also include a prescription for a sleeping pill for a couple of weeks until you've made some improvement in your sleep regime. Sleeping pills are not a long-term solution; they can lead to dependence and other side effects that include daytime drowsiness, which is just what you're trying to avoid. The most commonly prescribed sleeping pills are benzodiazepines (Ativan, Robinal, Valium). Over-the-counter sleep medications are antihistamines and they, too, have the side effect of daytime drowsiness. If conservative measures don't help, treatment with a low-dose tricyclic anti-depressant may help.

Although its sale is restricted in Canada, melatonin has gained a big following as an insomnia buster. This hormone, which is produced naturally in the body, is regulated by light and dark. The herbal remedy kava kava is an anti-anxiety treatment that is promoted as a sedative. It should not be used by someone suffering from depression or by pregnant or nursing mothers. (See What about Kava Kava?, page 193.) Valerian is another herbal remedy that may be effective as a sleep aid.

IT TAKES TWO

When one of you has a sleep problem, you both have to "own" the problem and decide to change. Both of you may have to change your expectations. For example, you may expect to go to bed together because that's your time to be intimate. But the advice to insomniacs is that they should go to bed only when they are sleepy, which may not be the same time as their partner. Together you need to discuss how you can separate meeting your needs for sex and intimacy from your needs for sleep.

You may also need to change your routines. People with insomnia should use their bedroom only for sleep and sex. That means the partner who doesn't have a problem sleeping needs to read and watch TV in the living or family room, not in the bedroom.

Sex is a great inducer of sleep, but sex that doesn't lead to orgasm can make sleep nearly impossible, observes sleep expert Paul Caldwell in his book *Sleep*. Anyone who has ever lain awake listening to the rhythmic breathing of a satisfied and sleeping spouse will attest to that. Sleep, when it does come, is lighter and interrupted by frequent waking. But relaxing, sensual touching like a massage can help you both sleep.

If you haven't found any relief after three months, ask for a referral to a sleep-disorder clinic. There are about a hundred of them across the country that specialize in chronic sleep disorders and their treatment. However, waiting lists can be long. (See Resources, page 282.)

Snoring

I was in a meeting recently with several women in their 40s. The subject of snoring came up and one woman described her and her partner's good night ritual. "It's smooch, smooch, good night, and then I pop in my earplugs." Another woman nodded in recognition and said that her earplugs are fluorescent pink so they glow in the dark. We all laughed, but not a lot. Although it's often treated as a joke, snoring isn't really that funny. It's rated as a serious problem in about one-third of marriages. And why wouldn't it be? Sleeping beside someone who snores disrupts a partner's sleep, leaving her (it's more often a her) irritable and chronically tired.

When someone who snores falls asleep, the muscles in the roof of the mouth (soft palate), tongue, and throat relax, partially obstructing his airway. As he breathes, the air causes the relaxed tissue to vibrate, which is what makes the noise. In people who also suffer from the related but more serious condition of sleep apnea, the airway is completely obstructed, which prevents them from breathing.

At age 35, only 20 per cent of men and 5 per cent of women snore. But by age 50, half of men and 30 per cent of women snore. Not surprisingly, as we baby boomers move through midlife and into our peak snoring years, a whole collection of anti-snoring devices is being patented and new laser surgery is available to reduce or eliminate snoring. But lifestyle changes should be your first line of defence. Being overweight is the most common cause of snoring.

Here's how to fight snoring the natural way:

❖ Lose weight. Even a few pounds can make a difference.
❖ Avoid alcohol and limit the use of antihistamines or sleeping pills, all of which affect the central nervous system and relax

the muscles even more. Sleep expert Paul Caldwell warns that these chemicals can turn a simple snoring problem into a sleep apnea problem.

❖ Sleep on your side. Sleeping on your back narrows your airway further. Try the old trick of sewing a tennis ball to the back of your pyjamas to keep you from rolling onto your back.

❖ Raise the head of the bed by 5 to 8 centimetres to open your airway more.

❖ Humidify the air in your bedroom. Dry air can irritate the nasal passageways and cause obstruction.

HOW BAD IS IT?

How to treat snoring depends on how loud it is. And the best person to measure that is the person who sleeps beside the snorer. The Mayo Clinic's sleep disorder centre has a grading system to rank snoring from the bed partner's point of view:

Grade 1: Heard only if you listen close to the face.
Grade 2: Heard in the room.
Grade 3: Heard just outside the bedroom with the door open.
Grade 4: Heard outside the bedroom with the door closed.

Decide that you deserve a good night's sleep no matter what decibel range your sleeping partner hits. Snorers are often embarrassed about the noise they make and would rather avoid discussing it, so their partners need to be direct and supportive about lifestyle changes that might help. Eating more low fat-food and exercising to lose weight may be good for both of you. Offer to go with your partner to the doctor to give your account of what's happening while he's asleep. Until the noise level goes

Talking about . . . sleep apnea solutions

Raoul, 52, and Cassie, 48, run their own cleaning supply business. They've been married for five years. It's his second marriage and her first. They live in Winnipeg, Manitoba. Raoul has two adult children from his first marriage.

Raoul: Before we were married, I was conscious of the fact that I didn't sleep very well. Sometimes I'd wake up and I couldn't get a breath. I was tired during the day, but I thought that being sleepy was part of midlife. I had no concept of what was happening.

Cassie: Raoul snored, so I spent my nights wearing earplugs. It was bearable. But I noticed that some time toward morning, he would occasionally gasp for breath and then snort. I knew he shouldn't be doing that, so I asked him to go to the doctor.

Raoul saw his family doctor (who thought he'd changed doctors because he hadn't been there in five years) and was eventually referred to a sleep lab. There he was diagnosed with mild-to-moderate sleep apnea, asked to lose 10 pounds (he was 10 per cent over his ideal weight) and given a continuous positive airway pressure (CPAP) machine to sleep with at night.

Raoul: I love it. It's a tremendous benefit. I had a choice of either a mask over the mouth or two little soft plugs that fit in each nostril [which he chose]. I would have been very uncomfortable with the mask. I had no problem adjusting, even the first night. I can do with less sleep now. I'm not sleepy like I used to be.

Cassie: His eyes would close around 9 at night, and if we had visitors it would be embarrassing. Now he can stay awake until 11 or later. Even with just the two of us, it's nice if someone can stay awake longer. It didn't disturb our intimacy. You can kiss before you put [the CPAP machine] on. Also, you can take it off quickly. The only problem was that cold air from the machine would blow down my neck. It was not pleasant. So we put two neck rolls between us. Raoul can still hug me. I like him to hold me around the tummy at night. I sleep better, too. All of a sudden it's quiet.

down, get yourself some earplugs, and move to a separate bedroom, even occasionally, to give yourself a chance to sleep well.

THE SURGERY OPTION

Laser surgery to trim the soft palate and the uvula (the little tag of flesh that hangs from the soft palate) removes some of the offending vibrating tissue to reduce or even eliminate the snoring noises. The surgery, called laser-assisted uvulopalatoplasty, is done in the doctor's office under the same local anesthetic as a dentist's freezing. Laser surgery is available at well over fifty clinics across the country. Most patients can drive themselves home after the procedure. Side effects include a moderate to severe sore throat for several days.

Sleep Apnea

The sawing noises of your partner's snoring go on and on and on – and then suddenly they stop. Several seconds, even a minute, go by and then you hear an explosive snort as his breathing resumes. That's sleep apnea, and it can be frightening to listen to at 2 a.m. Snorers are seldom aware that their airways can be completely obstructed over and over again during sleep. It's usually the snorer's bed partner who first suspects apnea and pushes for a visit to the doctor. The snorer will be aware that he feels extreme fatigue during the day as if he really didn't get much sleep night after night. In fact, he hasn't because his sleep has been interrupted each time he gasps for air.

Apnea typically affects overweight men over the age of 35. In women, it may begin after menopause. In recent years, sleep apnea has been linked to many serious cardiovascular illnesses, including hypertension, heart failure, heart attack, and stroke. But a systematic review of the research evidence done by five British researchers and published in the *British Medical Journal* in 1997 concluded that the relevance of sleep apnea to public health has been exaggerated and that the evidence to link apnea to heart disease was weak and contradictory. Much stronger evidence was found for a link between sleep apnea and daytime sleepiness and traffic accidents, however.

Being overweight and aging are definitely related to apnea, which begs the question whether apnea is a separate disease or whether it's a marker of obesity and getting older. Apnea is really tough on marriages. Living with someone who snores loudly all night and then is so tired during the day and evening that he or she has real trouble functioning can put stress on both partners. And, in fact, a small American study of apneics and their wives concluded that both husbands and wives were unhappy with their relationship.

Treating apnea involves a visit to a sleep disorder clinic to have tests that check your breathing while you sleep. Unfortunately, there are long waits at sleep clinics across the country. In British Columbia, for example, the wait can be up to one year. If apnea is diagnosed, then the first step can be lifestyle changes to lose weight and avoid alcohol and sleeping pills. Laser surgery may also be an option for mild to moderate apnea. (See The Surgery Option, page 150.) However, it's controversial because it may stop only the snoring, not the apnea. There are several mouth inserts on the market that move the jaw into a forward position to open the airway. Other solutions are continuous positive airway pressure (CPAP), which is a mask attached to a respirator that forces air into the mouth and nose, opening up the airway. It's cumbersome and can be uncomfortable enough that only about 40 per cent of users stick with it.

6

Exercise for Body and Mind

Just about every health problem that worries men and women in midlife can be prevented or reduced in gravity by regular physical activity.

Now here's a subject guaranteed to make two-thirds of us squirm – that's the proportion of Canadian men and women who are not active enough to maintain our health. In fact, if you're middle-aged you're probably less active than your parents are. A recent survey showed that 64-year-olds are more active than 35-year-olds.

You may have noticed that physical activity is mentioned in just about every section of this book – exercise to improve cardiovascular health, exercise to reduce menopause symptoms, exercise to improve sex, exercise to improve sleep and to reduce snoring. Just to be sure you know absolutely everything that exercise can do for you, here's the list from some organizations that promote physical activity to us.

What regular exercise can do for your heart and other organs, courtesy of the Heart and Stroke Foundation:

❖ Increases the amount of blood your heart can pump, which will give you more energy as more oxygen is delivered to your muscles.
❖ Lowers your resting heart rate. The heart will beat fewer times per minute and contract with greater force. This improves the efficiency of the heart so it doesn't have to work as hard.
❖ Lowers blood pressure, which reduces the strain on your heart.
❖ Lowers your risk of heart disease. This is due, in part, to reduced levels of LDL (bad cholesterol) and increased levels of

HDL (good cholesterol), which helps to protect against coronary heart disease.

❖ Increases your chance of surviving a heart attack by 20 per cent.

❖ Can improve a sluggish sex life by improving circulation, flexibility, energy, self-esteem, and body awareness. Improved heart and muscle fitness allows more blood to be pumped through the body. That's important because the arousal systems in men and women depend in part on blood circulation.

❖ Can contribute to the prevention of gout, a painful form of arthritis, and kidney stones by lowering levels of uric acid in your body.

❖ Improves the way your lungs work. Your breathing is improved as oxygen travels through your body more easily.

❖ Makes quitting smoking easier. Once you've made the commitment to get active, you won't want to tolerate the shortness of breath caused by cigarette smoking.

And from the Canadian Fitness and Lifestyle Institute, an organization whose mandate is to disseminate widely the scientific evidence for exercise, comes this list of benefits of physical activity in preventing or reducing the risk of other health problems:

Obesity – Exercise reduces the risk of weight gain.

Diabetes – Exercise helps prevent Type II diabetes. Also, the illness, when it does occur, can be controlled totally or in part with regular exercise and a nutrition program. A sedentary lifestyle makes diabetic symptoms and complications even worse.

Cancer – Active people tend to have a lower risk of colon cancer and breast cancer than sedentary people.

Mental disturbances – Being active reduces anxiety, tension, depression, and the need for psychotropic drugs, improves sleep quality, and induces relaxation.

Osteoporosis – Evidence suggests that exercise slows the rate of bone loss. Without exercise, bones tend to weaken with age.

Hormonal problems – There are growing indications that regular exercise helps retard the loss of hormone function. Growth hormone, a builder of lean tissue, decreases with age but is released during exercise in young and old alike. Cortisol, a stress-fighting hormone, tends to stay too long in the blood of older people. Physical activity helps to keep it down. A similar balance is imposed on insulin, the sugar-controlling hormone. Norepinephrine – the waistline-widening hormone – tends to be produced in abundance with age but can be kept in check with physical activity.

Arthritis – Physical activity can eliminate or reduce the need for pain medications in people with osteoarthritis. A lack of activity, on the other hand, increases the risk of osteoarthritic symptoms. Recent research on osteoarthritis suggests that lack of exercise aggravates joint pain and stiffness by allowing muscles to grow weaker and joints to become more painful.

Is Becoming Physically Active Your Patriotic Duty?

Active people help reduce national medical costs. The Conference Board of Canada, in conjunction with the Canadian Fitness and Lifestyle Research Institute, analyzed how increasing physical activity would reduce the costs of treating three illnesses – ischemic heart disease, colon cancer, and Type II diabetes. It concluded that a 1 per cent increase in the number of physically active adults would translate into more than $11 million in annual savings (in '93 dollars.) Sedentary Canadians are still in the majority, but their numbers are decreasing – from 79 per cent in 1981 to 63 per cent in 1995.

Talking about... family histories

Patsy, 42, an office manager, and Steven, 43, a stockbroker, have been married nineteen years. They live in Mississauga, Ontario. They have two children, ages 12 and 15.

Patsy: When I turned 40, I started thinking about what my mother went through in midlife. She had a hysterectomy, gained a lot of weight, and went into a depression. I wanted to be sure the same things didn't happen to me. I'd already been exercising for most of my life, but I went on a big self-improvement kick. I went to see a nutritionist and lost 15 pounds.

My husband's father died at 42 of a heart attack. In the last five years, my husband has gained 40 pounds. He has these four-hour lunches, and he probably drinks more than he should when he's out. There was an increase in his snoring, which was keeping me up. I'm entering peri-menopause, and for a few days before my period I have insomnia. So one night I got up in the middle of the night in a rage and wrote him a note. I told him I'm showing my love for my family by taking care of myself to be around for them. Ergo, he should, too. He doesn't care. He doesn't want to be around. I probably said some hurtful things. It's taken him a year and a half to make some lifestyle changes. He's seeing a nutritionist now.

Steven: I've outlived my father now. A friend passed away during the winter, and my golf went downhill last year. I realized that if I wanted to play golf, I'd have to lose some weight. And if there was a single catalyst for trying to make some changes, it was looking at the pictures of myself from our Florida holiday last year.

I went to see a nutritionist to talk about what foods I needed to change, and then tried to add in more exercise. The exercise part has been tough. It's been a month and I really haven't done anything significant. I've lost 14 pounds and have 45 to go. It's not all going to happen at once. You don't put on 45 pounds in a year, so you don't take it off that fast either.

If all that isn't enough encouragement, you're also likely to live longer if you exercise. Just about every health problem that worries men and women in midlife can be prevented or reduced in gravity by regular physical activity. So why aren't more of us active enough to reap these health benefits? The time crunch of the middle years is certainly one good excuse. But there must be other reasons. Think about why either you or your partner avoids physical activity, if you do. Here are some reasons I know about. I know some women who hate to sweat. It makes them feel unfeminine, somehow not in control. Or they are really afraid of hurting themselves, as if trying a new activity was a recipe for disaster. Some men feel foolish being physically active. "Real men shouldn't have to jog around the neighbourhood to get strong; they should already be strong, damn it." I know one guy who does heavy ladder work as part of his job. He probably could benefit from stretching out his back muscles but he'd feel silly. Artsy dancers stretch, guys who install satellite dishes don't. Then there are the people who are in denial. They start brisk walking, for instance, and find themselves out of breath after the first block. It's scary at age 40 to discover just how much ground you've lost. "Best to just forget the whole thing. I'll never manage to regain my 20-year-old prowess anyway."

A recent issue of *Health News* from the University of Toronto Faculty of Medicine looked at the problem of "exercise resistance" and pointed to the conscious or unconscious blocks to becoming regular exercisers. See if you recognize yourself in any of these common patterns of exercise resistance.

❖ You start a program, join a gym, or sign up for fitness classes with the best of intentions. But a few weeks later, you no longer feel any motivation to go and you quit. Then months later you start something else.

❖ You accept the evidence that there are health benefits to exercise but you don't see any personal relevance. You don't do any exercise and you have no intention of starting.

❖ The idea of exercising makes you feel hopeless, angry, and despairing. You dread it when someone – your spouse, your doctor, your teenage daughter – suggests you get more physically active. When you do try to be more active, you feel awkward, embarrassed, and anxious. You feel you should somehow be doing more.

What to Do

Figure out your personal excuses or blind spots and then figure out how to move beyond whatever is blocking you. Here are some suggestions:

Choose less loaded reasons – You already know that physical activity improves your health and contributes to weight loss, but if these aren't good motivators for you (or just make you feel more guilty or discouraged), then focus on reasons for exercise that do motivate you. One study of what motivates people to become more physically active has come to the simple conclusion that you will do it only if you enjoy it. Focus on spending time with your partner or a friend, on getting outside. Enjoy feeling less tired. Let the other benefits come with time.

Find out about the experience – Read about different kinds of physical activity and what they can do for you. Learn about how physical activity affects your body. Check out equipment, particularly the right kind of shoes for your activity. Talk to others who do activities you might like to try, and get pointers from them. The more information you have, the less intimidated you'll be.

Don't put all your exercise eggs in one basket – Try a variety of ways to get physical activity. Go to an aquafit class, make a date to bike with your neighbour, try out an exercise video, take a walk on your lunch break. These various activities will help you maintain your activity level in spite of vacations and the change of season.

Make a six-week plan and stick to it! – It takes six weeks to start feeling the physical and psychological benefits of physical activity. Start by setting goals you can reach and then follow through. If you lose your motivation, change activities but don't quit. If you hang in for six weeks, you have a good chance of beating your exercise resistance and becoming a lifelong exercise lover.

WHAT SHOULD YOU DO AND FOR HOW LONG?

I swear that nobody is paying me to say this, but Canadians have a wonderful new tool for deciding how to put more physical activity into their lives. It's called Canada's Physical Activity Guide to Healthy Active Living, brought to us by Health Canada and the Canadian Society for Exercise Physiology. Although it reads like a typical government brochure, it will revolutionize how you think about becoming more active.

The basic premise is that you need to accumulate 60 minutes of light physical activity every day to stay healthy. But the amount of time you spend depends on the amount of effort you expend. So as you progress to more vigorous activity, you can spend less time – 30 minutes a day, four times a week. At its lightest, that activity would make you feel a little warm and you'd notice a slight increase in breathing. As you progressed to more effort, you'd feel warmer, breathing would be more rapid. At a level of vigorous effort – jogging, for example – you would be quite warm and breathing would be very rapid.

This physical activity can be done in 10-minute chunks – just as long as it all adds up to 60 minutes of light effort (or 30 minutes of vigorous effort) every day. What is wonderful about the concept is that it looks at physical activity in the context of your day-to-day life, rather than as an exercise routine that you need to shoehorn into your already very busy waking hours.

Although the guide mentions all three forms of activity – endurance for heart and lungs, flexibility for muscles and joint mobility, and strength activities for building muscles and bones – the emphasis is on endurance activities because this is usually where those who are sedentary and who have the most to gain by becoming active will derive the most benefit.

The Health Canada group who worked on this handbook for several years took Canada's Food Guide to Healthy Eating as their model. Just as the Food Guide gives us a common-sense approach to incorporating healthy food choices into our meals, rather than a diet to follow slavishly, the Physical Activity Guide gives us an approach with flexibility and realistic expectations. The examples in the case studies include single moms who do "ab" exercises by tightening muscles on the bus ride home from work, and guys who walk 10 minutes at lunch as part of their 60 minutes. Do not pass go. Call 1-888-334-9769 or visit www.paguide.com for your copy today. It's free.

SPUR EACH OTHER ON

Some couples find that exercising together helps them to maintain their commitment, when they find activities they both enjoy. Decide what works best for both of you. Christopher and I tried running together but stopped because he sets a faster pace than I do, and I was slowing him down. But we can match our pace more easily when we're walking together or cross-country skiing

Talking about... working out together

*Karen, 39, a homemaker, and Newman, 32, a computer programmer, have
been married for a year. They live in rural Ontario. They have no children.
They quit smoking and began walking together after Karen was diagnosed
with fibromyalgia. Walking has given her more stamina.*

Karen: At first, I'd say, "Are you ready for our walk?" And he'd say, "Again?"
I've gone for walks by myself and I don't enjoy it so much. It's much nicer
together – we talk all the time. People have said to me that I'm really lucky
that my husband will go for walks with me. I suppose I am. It's just what we
do together – Mostly we go at a fast pace, but on the weekends we stop in
the little shops downtown. Now we jog about half a kilometre during our
walk. My goal is to walk to Elora and back. It's about a ten-kilometre round
trip. We'll walk there, have a beer, and walk back. I think we will have earned
that beer.

Newman: Initially, the walking was something she needed to do after
she got sick. Walking together was a conscious decision we made to help
her feel better. After a while, we both wanted to go. We spur each other on.
My job is mentally stressful and when I get home I'm tired, but we always
end up going for our walk. When I did exercise on my own, it wasn't terribly
exciting, but when you're together you're more motivated. I find it difficult
when I travel. I'm glad to get home and get back to our fitness routine.

Karen: It was six to eight weeks before I noticed anything. At first, I
could just go for the walk and sometimes I'd be too tired to make dinner.
What it's done for me is that I can go for the walk and do a whole pile of
things the same day. I still have flare-ups of fibromyalgia when I don't feel
very good for a couple of days, but that's normal.

in the winter. If he gets ahead of me, we just meet back at the chalet. Whether you actually exercise together or not, make a pact of mutual support so that each of you accepts the other's commitment to living an active life.

HOW CAN EXERCISE PREVENT AGING?

But what if you're part of the one-third who are already active? In midlife, should you expect a slow decline of strength? Not necessarily. I found it ironic that I wrote this section the same day that Wayne Gretzky played his last hockey game. At 38, in early middle age, his body was telling him that it was time to stop pushing its limits. As we sat glued to the television watching Wayne cry, I could imagine all those other middle-aged Canadians crying with a personal sense of loss. If it's over for Gretzky, is it over for us, too, except nobody's giving us the Mercedes? But elite athletes like Gretzky live by different rules than the rest of us because they push their bodies to maximum effort each time they hit the ice or the running track in a competitive situation. In hockey they also push their limits by throwing themselves into the boards and into each other a few dozen times a game. We may love to applaud their efforts, but they're not doing their bodies any favours over the long haul.

There is a group of athletes who can give us an example of what's possible through midlife. These are Masters athletes, who train vigorously and continue to compete within their age group throughout their lives. Masters sports include running, swimming and cycling – no body checking. In his book *Aging, Physical Activity, and Health* (Human Kinetics Publishers, 1997), Roy J. Shephard, professor emeritus at the University of Toronto, describes a study of Masters athletes. The group studied maintained a training schedule four times per week of approximately

50 minutes per session for men and 40 minutes for women from their 20s to their 70s. Moving through midlife had little effect on their performance. Their training speeds and the length of their sessions remained relatively constant until their eighth decade, when both speeds and times dropped off. Similarly, their level of body fat showed little increase and their percentage of lean tissue stayed the same until their 70s, unlike their sedentary counterparts. We're not all cut out to become Masters athletes, but studies like this one point to the idea that what we accept as aging – the rubber tire, the lack of muscle tone – is really lack of physical activity. The middle years of life do not automatically mean loss of physical prowess. And you can be sure that while Wayne won't be getting bashed into the boards anymore, he also won't be giving up the training that's given him his edge until now. And I bet Janet's no slouch in the training department either.

What we accept as aging – the rubber tire, the lack of muscle tone – is really lack of physical activity.

Exercise Your Mind

An editor I know was telling me that she was noticing little memory slips – she couldn't remember whether she'd actually left a message for a writer the day before about an assignment or whether she just thought she had. That same day she'd forgotten where she'd left her car in a parking lot. She blamed her age in a joking way. But underneath her light tone I could hear the edge of fear that most of us in midlife understand. Is forgetting where your car is at 50 the slippery slope to forgetting where your house is at 70? In fact, the fear of mental degeneration may be the greatest terror of midlife.

It's an understandable fear, given how little we really know about the distinctions between what are normal changes that occur in the brain through aging and the changes that signal the onset of neurodegenerative diseases such as Alzheimer's disease or Parkinson's disease. Scientists tell us that very few people in midlife are affected by neurodegenerative disease. Studies show that among seniors 65 and older, only a small percentage have some form of cognitive illness. With age, the numbers increase. Between 65 and 74, about 2 per cent have cognitive impairment; between 75 and 84, 17 per cent have some impairment, and after age 85, 37 per cent do. For the majority of people, midlife is a period of sharp focus and mental ability – not a period of observable loss. But nobody knows for sure whether there are connections between the changes that everyone experiences in midlife and the experience of neurodegenerative disease in old age.

Dozens of books are devoted to the idea that you can influence how your brain ages and improve your memory and mental acuity by following a certain diet, reducing stress, getting enough physical activity and sleep, and avoiding substances such as alcohol, cigarettes, and marijuana. Inasmuch as having a healthy body means having a healthy brain, the advice makes sense (and I'll share some of it later on in this section). But David Mann of the department of pathological sciences at the University of Manchester, in his book *Sense and Senility: The Neuropathology of the Aged Human Brain* (Chapman & Hall, 1997), points to recent research that suggests that inheriting good genes may have the most influence on how well your brain ages.

So much about our understanding of the brain has changed in recent years. Take, for instance, something as simple as the accepted wisdom that the brain shrinks with age. Mann explains that this shrinkage may have been exaggerated because it didn't account for changes in body size over the last hundred years. Just as our bodies are bigger now because of improved nutrition, so too our brains are bigger. Your grandmother, born at the beginning of the twentieth century, started out with a smaller brain to begin with, for whatever that's worth.

We have to leave it to the neuroscientists to figure out the connection between the normal brain changes of middle adulthood and the neurodegenerative diseases that may occur in old age. What we know, however, is what changes to expect in our memory function as we move through middle age. Psychologist Angela Troyer of Baycrest Centre for Geriatric Care in Toronto, an expert on memory and aging, offers this description: "Our memory abilities increase through childhood and peak in our late teens or early 20s. And then from there is a very gradual, constant decline throughout adulthood. Most of us don't notice the slight changes in our 30s, but by our 40s and 50s, we're likely to notice some memory changes. By our 60s and 70s, the changes become more noticeable." According to Troyer, here's what to expect:

MEMORY TYPE	DEFINITION	EXAMPLES WITH AGE	CHANGE
Semantic memory	The accumulation of facts and experience you gain over your lifetime	Building your vocabulary	Stability or improvement with age
Immediate memory	The ability to remember what happened a few seconds ago	Remembering a telephone number just after looking it up	Very slight decline with age
Recent memory	The ability to remember what happened minutes, hours, or days ago	Remembering the name of someone you met two days ago	Moderate decline with age
Remote memory	The ability to remember things that happened years ago	Remembering details from your childhood	Relative stability with age
Prospective memory	The ability to remember to do something in the future	Remembering to go to an appointment	Decline (without cues), but stable (with cues)

So my friend who couldn't find her car was experiencing a typical "recent memory" loss. But how much that had to do with her age and how much it had to do with what else was happening in her life is a question. She might have just been stressed out or over-tired. Stress affects your ability to concentrate and to make deci-sions. You don't process information so you can't recall it. Lack of sleep and interrupted sleep also affect your memory. If your sleep is interrupted during REM sleep when dreaming occurs, it may also affect your memory of the previous day's events. There are a variety of medical and physical changes that can negatively affect memory. According to Troyer, they are:

❖ thyroid problems
❖ depression and anxiety
❖ cardiovascular disease
❖ medications for depression, high blood pressure, allergies.

Also, some women experience slight memory lapses during the hormonal changes related to menopause.

HEALTHY BODY, HEALTHY BRAIN

The best way to maintain your memory is to maintain your over-all health. Physical activity also has at least a short-term effect on memory. After you exercise, you perform better on memory tests, Troyer says. And continuing to learn and being open to new ideas and activities will keep your memory sharper.

Just worrying about your memory can make matters worse. Troyer says that many of the middle-aged people who attend her Memory and Aging workshop say that what's most comforting is being able to talk with others about their fears and their experi-ences. "Memory changes aren't like getting grey hair or glasses.

You can't see that other people are experiencing the same kinds of changes. That's why it's important to talk about them," she says.

TALK TO EACH OTHER

Being married is probably good for your memory. Research on cognitive ability shows that married people have a slower rate of decline with aging. Troyer speculates that being married means that you have someone to share new activities with: "If you have a spouse who likes to travel, you're likely to do it as well." New activities make you mentally sharper and improve your memory.

You also build memories together. Nobody's memory is perfect. Rather, all memory is filled with errors and gaps. And your memory is not just what's in your own head. "Memory is more of a cooperative, interactive effort," Troyer says. So you each have bits of memories and interpretations of events and you can correct each other's errors and fill in each other's gaps. (You can also get into battles royal about who exactly decided to buy that mutual fund that's just taken a nosedive or whose idea it was anyway to paint the dining room chartreuse, but that's another issue.)

HAVE GOOD HABITS FOR A GOOD MEMORY

We forget things because we're rushing, overloaded with tasks, and trying to do too much. Instead of relying on your overburdened memory, develop some simple habits instead. Here are some tips from Troyer:

Always losing your keys or your glasses? – Decide on a logical spot to keep them and get into the habit of putting them there.

Missing upcoming appointments? – Write the event down and make it a habit to check your calendar regularly. Or if you're deep into a project at work and are afraid you'll forget a 3 o'clock meeting, set the alarm on your watch to remind you.

Never remember a name? – Pay close attention when you first hear the name. Repeat the name several times. Make the name meaningful, using definitions, visualization, or association with someone you know.

Never remember a phone number? – Write it down. Look for patterns. Repeat it to yourself several times.

Get to the mall and can't remember everything you need? – So make a list. Organize it into meaningful clusters.

Can't remember all the details you'd like about a past event? – Keep track of your life in a journal. Reread entries regularly.

WHAT HAPPENS TO INTELLIGENCE IN MIDLIFE?

Not much, as it turns out. Intelligence is understood to be a combination of several factors. Your "fluid" intelligence is your capacity to process information. Your "crystallized" intelligence is your knowledge based on your life experience. As you might expect, fluid intelligence goes down throughout adult life and crystallized intelligence goes up. The combination of the two, called omnibus intelligence, stays about the same, at least until you reach your 60s.

IQ tests have been used to identify how intelligence changes with age, but their use is controversial; they are a blunt instrument at best. For example, IQ scores increase with levels of education. Today's 20-year-olds had a much better education on average than today's 50-year-olds had. So the better IQ scores of the 20-year-olds may reflect their level of education more than their higher intellectual abilities.

There is no evidence that your ability to learn new skills is hampered as you age. What you need to think about through midlife is your attitude to learning. Misconceptions about your ability to learn can be self-fulfilling. Realize that you have different intellectual abilities in midlife than you had at 20 and capitalize on them.

7

Breaking Bad Habits

*A supportive spouse, especially one who has
gone through the same process, makes a
major difference to the other partner's
success in quitting smoking.*

My husband, Christopher, and I recently attended a 50th birthday party for an old high school friend. Everybody stood cheek by jowl in the kitchen and living room talking and laughing; the bar set up in the downstairs family room was much quieter. The few smokers in the group disappeared out onto the back deck occasionally for a cigarette. Several of us there had been friends since our teens. I couldn't help but be struck by how our parties had changed in 30 years – the beer didn't flow as freely, there wasn't a pair of bell-bottoms in sight, and there was no blue haze of cigarette smoke hanging over the group. We did, however, crank up the Led Zeppelin at one point.

On average, we drink and smoke less as we age, which, as Martha Stewart would say, is a good thing. Tobacco is lethal at any age, and alcohol, while it can actually be beneficial in small amounts, can also have a more serious health impact in midlife.

So You're Still Smoking

Let's skip the list of tobacco evils, shall we, and get to the main issue: What are the best quitting methods for someone who has been smoking for fifteen to twenty years or longer and wants to give it up?

You have to believe, first of all, that quitting is possible. That's difficult to do if you're still smoking, because you've probably tried to quit at least once. The Centre for Addiction and

Talking about . . . quitting together

Karen, 39, a homemaker, and Newman, 32, a computer programmer, have been married for a year. They live in rural Ontario. They have no children. They quit smoking and began walking together after Karen was diagnosed with fibromyalgia. Quitting smoking together helped both of them.

Karen: I was smoking two packs a day. I tried quitting once before, but I went back to it. When I started making bread by hand, I got winded after a couple of minutes. You're not supposed to get winded two minutes into kneading bread! I knew that wasn't good. And I have blood pressure problems. I decided I wanted to start walking. Smoking and walking aren't too compatible, and I just kept telling myself over and over that smoking makes me sick . I started cutting down, and since Newman only smoked at home when I did, he cut down, too. Quitting together is essential, I think. I can't imagine smelling it [when you're trying to quit]. When I first quit, if I'd pass someone who was smoking, I'd just want to follow them.

Newman: I've smoked on and off for twenty years. Maybe less than a pack a month, but I'd quit for a couple of weeks, then always go back. Quitting smoking with a partner makes a difference. You want to prolong your life together. You think, God, I need a smoke, but you always have to remember that you're better without it. Now it's no longer an issue. If I smell smoke, I can't stand it. And I think she's getting to be the same.

Mental Health (formerly the Addiction Research Foundation) has a great statistic in its literature that might give you some hope: half of all Canadians who ever smoked have now quit.

Unfortunately, there is no magic bullet yet. Zyban, the latest smoking cessation drug on the market, has a reported success rate of 23 per cent of study participants staying smoke-free after 12 months. And that was in a study where one-third of participants dropped out.

Most smokers who quit do it on their own, cold turkey. But not after the first try. The majority who quit try several times before they succeed. Try again and think of quitting smoking as a step-by-step process. Use whatever methods work for you. If you do start smoking again, don't give up. Figure out what *did* work in your previous attempts and what went wrong, then prepare to try again when you're ready. Even a short break without cigarettes is good for your body. The carbon dioxide levels in your bloodstream go down within a few hours, and after three days, your lung capacity shows improvement.

Blech!

Withdrawal symptoms, especially in the first two days:

❖ cravings and thinking about smoking all the time

❖ trouble concentrating, feeling tense and irritable

❖ feeling dizzy, shaky, headaches

❖ coughing

❖ constipation or an upset stomach

❖ tingling or numbness in arms and legs

❖ food cravings, especially for sweets

Source: Heart and Stroke Foundation of Canada

Planning for quitting is an important element for some people. You set a date in the future to quit, being careful to choose a time when you won't be under stress. Then you might make changes to your smoking routine – cutting back, changing to a lighter brand, not smoking in certain areas of your house or in your car – to prepare for quitting altogether.

Talking about . . . not quitting together

Cindy, 41, a waitress, and George, 43, a plumber, have been married fifteen years. They live in Red Deer, Alberta. They have two children, ages 11 and 13. They've discussed quitting smoking for several years but haven't managed it together. George quit on his own a year ago, using the medication Zyban.

George: I wanted to quit, but I didn't tell her one way or the other. I just talked to the doctor and started taking the medication. Then I guess I told her what was going on. I asked her to try, too, because it would be easier for me to quit if she quit. She said she was going to quit eventually, but she wasn't ready to quit now. So she started to smoke on the front porch or outside. If I'm home, she smokes outside. If I'm not home and it's just her and the kids, she smokes inside. We've also talked about the fact that it's not good for the kids. They are always bugging us not to smoke in front of them.

Every now and again, it smells good, like I'd like to have one. Actually after I had quit smoking, I found half a cigarette on the porch one day and I smoked that. Then I thought, What the hell am I doing that for? I smoked it, but I didn't have another one. But a few times I had to think about it again and read the pamphlet over.

I've stopped snoring since I quit smoking. I mentioned to her that her snoring keeps me awake now that I don't snore. She says, "Too bad."

And another thing, the ashtrays really stink. When I walk in the front porch at night, it really stinks. For thirty years, it didn't bother me. Now I quit and everything bothers me. But I've stopped saying anything. I realize that's not going to get me anywhere. I really can't see her quitting any time soon.

Cindy: If he wants to quit, that's up to him. I just think that until a person is ready to quit, she won't get anywhere with it. I could say to him that I'm going to quit because he has bugged me about it. I may not smoke in the house, but as soon as I get out of the house, I'll light one. Quitting smoking is pretty personal. You have to be ready. When I took up walking, he didn't come with me. I do appreciate the fact that he has quit. I think it's great that he has quit. I think it's wonderful, considering he smoked 2½ packs a day. I'm really amazed. It's also made me cut down a lot. A package of cigarettes now lasts me two days. It helps. So when I do decide to quit, it won't be quite as difficult.

OTHER TRICKS THAT CAN HELP

- ❖ Reward yourself. Put aside the money you save by not buying cigarettes. Plan to spend it on a holiday or some other treat for yourself.
- ❖ Start some physical activity you enjoy. Keep it simple and easy, such as going for a regular walk. When you feel physically fitter, you can keep your spirits up. It can also help to minimize weight gain, although the average gain is only 2 or 3 kilograms (4 to 6 pounds).
- ❖ Keep a diary of your quitting process. Include a list of your reasons for quitting. Record your urges, what worked, what didn't. You'll learn by your successes and by your mistakes.
- ❖ You may want to enlist the support of others in your battle. One study shows that a supportive spouse, especially one who has gone through the same process, makes a major difference to the other partner's success in quitting.
- ❖ Talk to your family doctor about your plans. You may want to try Zyban, which requires a prescription, or the nicotine patch or gum, which are available over the counter. Bupropion hydrochloride (Zyban) works directly on the chemicals in the brain that may affect nicotine addiction. Nicotine patches and gum replace nicotine from cigarettes, thereby reducing your cravings. Your doctor should also be supportive rather than "preachy." When researchers asked a group of current smokers and others who had recently quit how they felt about their doctors' help, many said they felt overloaded with health information about the dangers of smoking. They said they didn't need to be reminded. Some, who weren't ready to quit, said they avoided visiting their doctor for other reasons because they didn't want an anti-smoking lecture. You already know that smoking is the biggest threat to your health and that quitting is your major health challenge. Find a

doctor who can help you with the task rather than make you feel guilty.

❖ There are dozens of quit-smoking groups you can join that may help you. Be skeptical of the claims of high success rates from some of the commercial organizations since few are based on any rigorous research. But as long as you're not blowing a load of money you can't afford, joining a group might help. Check with your family doctor, your local Heart and Stroke Foundation, The Lung Association, Canadian Cancer Society, hospital or public health department for programs available. Good luck.

Would You Like a Drink?

For the majority of Canadian adults the answer is yes, at least on occasion. As a couple, you may have what some researchers call a drinking partnership. Your pattern of alcohol consumption is influenced by your relationship. For example, studies show that men and women drink less after they marry, possibly because married couples tend to do different kinds of social activities, like having another couple over for dinner, which in turn becomes "Come for supper and bring the kids."

A 1998 study published in the *Journal of Marriage and the Family* examined a wide variety of couples' drinking patterns and how they affected marriage quality. Not surprisingly, heavy drinking patterns weren't good for relationships. When husbands and wives either drank alcohol together or apart, the pattern was not necessarily detrimental to their relationship. However, in couples who drank frequently and together, the women consumed the same amount of alcohol as their husbands, and above the average for their gender.

HOW MUCH IS TOO MUCH?

With all the recent emphasis on the cardiovascular benefits of moderate alcohol consumption, particularly for men over 35 and women past menopause, you'd be forgiven for thinking that a daily drink was an absolute must in midlife. It isn't. Remember that there are other non-alcoholic ways to benefit your heart, such as more physical activity, a low-fat diet, and avoiding tobacco. One drink every other day is enough to reap the cardiovascular benefits. And that drink does *not* need to be red wine. It's the alcohol itself that offers the protection.

Balanced against this new research about the benefits of alcohol to heart health is the reality that over-consumption increases your risk of high blood pressure and may increase the risk of breast cancer in women. The margin of error between the benefits and risks of drinking is very small. So you need to understand what the experts mean by moderation. Here are the latest guidelines for alcohol consumption from the Centre for Addiction and Mental Health.

❖ Limit your weekly intake to 14 or fewer standard drinks for men and 9 or fewer standard drinks for women.

❖ Drink no more than 2 standard drinks on any day. (Even if you stay within the weekly guidelines, drinking more than 2 drinks a day can be detrimental. And binge drinking – more than 5 drinks at one time – accelerates atherosclerosis and raises blood pressure and may involve additional risks, such as injuries.)

❖ Drink slowly to avoid intoxication, waiting at least an hour between drinks and taking alcohol with food and non-alcoholic beverages.

A standard drink is defined as one 341 mL (12 oz) bottle of beer (5% alcohol), one 142 mL (5 oz) glass of table wine (12% alcohol), or one 43 mL (1½ oz) shot of liquor (40% alcohol).

The people who should not use alcohol or should limit their use to less than these maximum amounts are:

* people with health problems, such as liver disease or psychiatric illnesses
* people taking medications, such as sedatives, sleeping pills, and pain killers
* people with a personal or family history of serious drinking problems
* women who are pregnant, trying to conceive, or breast-feeding.

And, of course, anyone who is driving any kind of vehicle or working with machinery, or who is restricted from drinking shouldn't be drinking.

Although women are less likely than men to develop alcohol problems, they are more vulnerable to the effects of alcohol in several ways. Women's bodies absorb alcohol more quickly, so they feel the effects of alcohol faster. They also develop health problems from alcohol at much lower consumption levels than men. A recent issue of the University of Toronto *Health News* reported that "research suggests that women who consume an average of 3 or more drinks a day develop health problems which don't show up in male drinkers until their average daily consumption reaches 9 drinks." These problems include hepatitis, cirrhosis of the liver, and damage to the nervous system, especially the brain.

Finally, alcohol affects both of you more as you age because your tolerance decreases. So enjoy a cold one after a long day or a glass of wine with dinner – just don't make it three.

Stress and Depression

The good news is that midlife is a time of increasing sense of control. The bad news is that for many men and women, early midlife – the 10 years between age 35 and 45 – can be their most demanding and stressful years.

"I'm tired all the time and life is no longer fun. I wonder which came first and whether I'm now clinically depressed or just overwhelmed with responsibilities." This was how one woman in a recent survey on fatigue described her situation. Although she didn't use the word *stress*, if someone had asked her whether she felt under stress, she probably would have said that she was. The links she makes between being tired, perhaps being depressed, and being overwhelmed will resonate with most people at some point in their lives. And when hormonal changes get added to the mix, it gets tough to figure out just what's getting you down.

The good news is that for many, midlife is a time of increasing sense of control over their lives. The bad news is that for many men and women, early midlife – the ten years between age 35 and 45 – can be their most demanding and stressful years.

Stress, fatigue, and depression are all tied up together; to deal with one of them you need to address one or all of the others. And just as you both benefit from establishing goals for common food and sleep issues, so you'll benefit from learning together how to manage your stress and improve your moods. Clinical depression is an illness that requires medical treatment. But you can sometimes prevent depression by reducing fatigue, negative stress reactions, and bad moods before they spiral down into full-blown depression.

Too Tired to Care

Fatigue can be a byproduct of stress; it's also a classic symptom of depression. But not getting enough sleep may mean that you handle stress badly and may make you more prone to depression. It's tough to figure out what comes first. Some people are so used to being tired that they don't even know what it feels like to be well rested anymore. In a study conducted by Dr. Donna Stewart, the chair of women's health at the Toronto Hospital, and her colleagues, fatigue was women's top health concern. Fatigue is also one of the major complaints of men in midlife. Focus on *getting enough sleep* as your first step toward reducing your stress levels and protecting yourselves against depression. (See Sleep, Chapter 5.)

Stress

It isn't your age that predicts your stress level. Rather, it's the events that happen during a particular time in your life. For many people, early midlife is a period of multiple roles and many demands, but if you are in your early 40s and you have two small kids, a precarious job, and an ailing parent, you'll be under much more stress than if you were in your early 40s with your kids already launched, a secure job, and healthy parents.

By the time you've reached midlife you know something about what your stressors are and how you cope with them. You probably also know what stresses your partner and how he or she copes. If you're not sure, it's worth comparing notes. Stress is difficult to discuss because we each have different ideas about what the word *stress* means. We may use it to mean an external event – losing a job, getting caught in a traffic jam. Or we use it to describe our response to an event – a racing heart, an upset stomach. But what really defines stress is how you personally react to an event. One person's major stress event is another person's piece of cake.

STAGES OF STRESS

The stages of stress are described neatly in a booklet "Coping with Stress" put out by the Heart and Stroke Foundation and the Canadian Mental Health Association.

In response to stressful events, you can experience one, two, or all of the following stages:

Stage 1: Mobilization of Energy

All bodily activity is increased in response to a stressor that is frightening, such as a near car accident. Such a stressor starts the body's "fight-flight" reaction, causing the release of adrenaline. You feel your heart pounding and your palms feel sweaty. This is called primary stress.

This reaction can also be the result of stressful situations that you choose. This is called secondary stress.

Symptoms
* increased heart rate and blood pressure
* rapid breathing
* sweating
* decreased digestion rate, which feels like butterflies and indigestion

Stage 2: Exhaustion or Consuming Energy

If there is no escape from Stage 1, the body will begin to release stored sugars and fats, using up its bodily resources.

Symptoms
  ❖ feeling driven
  ❖ feeling pressured
  ❖ tiredness and fatigue
  ❖ increase in smoking, caffeine and/or alcohol consumption
  ❖ anxiety
  ❖ memory loss
  ❖ acute illnesses such as colds and flu

Stage 3: Draining Energy Stores
If the stressful situation is not resolved, you may become chronically stressed. The body's need for energy resources exceeds its ability to produce them.

Symptoms
Serious illness, including:
  ❖ heart disease
  ❖ mental illness such as depression

As well as:
  ❖ errors in judgment
  ❖ personality changes

The effects of stress are cumulative, eventually leading to serious health consequences if you aren't able to reduce the stress or to improve your coping skills.

Men and women may react differently to stress. There is some evidence that women don't take as much responsibility for dealing with their stress as men do, that they tend to put another's needs or desires ahead of their own to the point of jeopardizing their own health. So instead of planning for some relaxation in the form of exercise or socializing, they keep running from the kids' hockey games to grocery shopping to work with no down time. However, many women in midlife have more caregiving roles than men – both for kids and for older relatives. Eventually something has to give.

HOW TO DISAGREE

The quality of your relationship affects your stress levels and therefore your health. Research shows that what distinguishes happy and presumably less stressful marriages from unhappy ones is how disagreements are resolved. Couples in strong relationships have disagreements but also methods for resolving those disagreements. Couples in poor relationships get locked in discussions that escalate into power struggles, with each partner fighting for the upper hand. Studies have shown that marital conflict has a negative effect on the immune system, even in healthy adults. Women are more likely than men to show physiological effects from these conflicts.

If the way you resolve problems together makes your blood pressure spike, you need to find better ways to tackle your conflicts. But it should be noted that even bad problem solving is better than no problem solving at all. Couples experience the most long-term stress in their marriages when they don't express feelings of anger.

JUST DEAL WITH IT

Every man and every woman has stress. It's how you deal with it that counts. You can help each other handle stress by being available to go for a walk together or by having a laugh together to break the tension. Here's a collection of good ideas to get you started:

1. Learn to recognize your signs of stress. One man I know says that when he catches himself snapping at his kids, he knows he's under stress. Irritability, losing your sense of humour, and difficulty concentrating are all signs that stress has you in its grip. Of course, physical signs such as a churning stomach are also strong indicators.

2. Take a mini-break. Give yourself five minutes to go for a walk, do a few stretches, listen to a couple of songs on the CD player, or have a cold drink. Learn to break the action for a few minutes every couple of hours.

3. Stick to your routine. How are you sleeping? Eating? When you're under stress, it's easy to skip meals or cut into sleep to finish a project. Don't do it. You can't be effective if you don't take care of your basic needs.

4. Deal with your time problems. We all have them. Some of us over-schedule, others can't delegate or never allocate enough time to finish a task. Figure out what your time glitches are and solve them. Get a calendar agenda and use it. Make it automatic to ask "Who else can help?" when you're in a time crunch. Decide how long a task should take and then add extra time to be sure.

5. Learn relaxation techniques like deep breathing, yoga, and meditation.

6. Get physical. Physical activity is probably the best instant stress reliever. Walk around the shop floor. Take the kids for a walk in the park. A regular routine of exercise will also make you more resilient to stress reactions in the first place.

7. Laugh. It may be the last thing you feel like doing, but it works. Studies show it releases stress-relieving chemicals in the brain. Put a joke book in your desk drawer at work. Tape some "Seinfeld" reruns for emergencies. Diffuse a tense discussion with a silly crack.

8. Socialize. Call a friend and talk over what's bothering you. Chat with a neighbour. Play with your dog.

9. Plan for pleasure. When you plan your day, schedule in time for the activities you enjoy – a half hour to read a novel, time to garden, a shopping break at lunch hour. When you do long-term planning, plan a vacation that you know you will enjoy. Make your pleasure as high a priority as your obligations.

10. Change your style. If you're argumentative, try avoiding arguments; if you're a "superwoman" or "superman," start saying no; if you're a perfectionist, aim for "good enough" on occasion.

11. Throw away the crutches. If being stressed out for you means that you "need" a cigarette, a drink, a joint, yet another cup of coffee, or a bowl of ice cream, then rethink your strategy. Using any of these crutches to relieve stress may give you short-term relief but you'll pay later. There's always the real danger of sliding into more serious substance abuse problems.

Strategies for Stress Management

In a study of Canadian ethnic minority women who were asked about their stress management strategies, the most frequently mentioned stress relievers were:

- ❖ prayer
- ❖ listening to music
- ❖ a hot bath
- ❖ exercise and reading (ranked equally)
- ❖ positive affirmations

WHAT ABOUT KAVA KAVA?

Kava kava is a traditional herb from the islands of the South Pacific, where it's drunk to produce feelings of relaxation and a sense that all is right with the world. In North America, it's sold as an anti-anxiety drug and relaxant. However, kava kava is not recommended if you are suffering from depression, and women who are pregnant or nursing should not use it. The Commission E in Germany, which has studied the drug, has approved it for use since 1990. It recommended a daily dose of 60 to 120 mg of kavalactones (the active ingredient) and that the herb not be taken for more than three months without consulting a doctor. Side effects can include upset stomach and allergic reactions. Larger doses can cause intoxication and have been shown to cause skin rashes, visual disturbances, and balance problems.

Depression

Depression can strike you out of the blue or it can occur as a reaction to a series of difficulties or stresses, such as the death of a parent or a financial crisis. Experiencing too many stressors at once – your company is facing a buyout, your mother has just had a heart attack, and your teenage son is coming home drunk on the weekends – can put you over the edge. Some of us may be predisposed to depression, either because of a family history, or a brain chemical abnormality, or the traumas that have occurred in our lives. For example, having lost a parent early in life or having been sexually abused can make you more prone to depression. Although depression can be caused by life events, it's also recognized as a biological illness brought on by an imbalance in brain chemistry that can be treated with medication and with other therapies.

Women are more susceptible to depression than men; one-quarter of women and about half as many men suffer from depression at least once in their lives. Nobody knows for sure why women suffer more depression than men, but the phenomenon is worldwide. Dr. Donna Stewart, who conducted the fatigue study (page 188), says that women point to social factors as the sources of stress, fatigue, and depression. These women, who see themselves as caregivers responsible for everyone else's well-being, take on so many functions for others that they become overwhelmed and so stressed that they become depressed. Other researchers point out that women experience many hormonal fluctuations during menstruation, pregnancy, and menopause, which may affect brain chemistry.

Although depression is often referred to as the "common cold" of mental illnesses, it's an illness that's hard for both sufferer and doctor to recognize. Many people either don't want to admit they have it or they don't realize that their cluster of symptoms has a name. However, once depression is recognized, it can be successfully treated, especially with the newer medications, such as selective seratonin reuptake inhibitors (SSRIs).

HOW TO DECIDE WHETHER YOU'RE FEELING LOW OR YOU'RE CLINICALLY DEPRESSED

Deciding whether what you're feeling is a temporary case of the blues or clinical depression can be difficult. Often one's partner suspects depression before the person suffering from the depression does. The symptoms are:

- ❖ feelings of sadness and loss of interest or pleasure that last more than two weeks
- ❖ changes in sleep patterns, especially waking early, at 3 or 4 a.m.
- ❖ feeling slowed down and without energy
- ❖ fatigue
- ❖ filled with self-blame and feelings of guilt
- ❖ difficulties concentrating
- ❖ feeling agitated or restless
- ❖ feeling defeated with nothing to live for.

If you suspect that you are depressed, don't wait to get help. Most depressions eventually lift but may take months to do so. Call your family physician to discuss your concerns. He or she can assess your mood and decide whether you are clinically depressed. If you are, he or she will probably prescribe an anti-depressant. The medication may be one of the selective seratonin reuptake inhibitors (SSRIs), of which Prozac is the most well known. Other SSRIs include Zoloft and Fluvox. These drugs work in the brain to maintain optimal levels of seratonin. You should feel some relief within a few weeks. If not, your doctor may try another medication until you find one that works for you. The SSRIs are the most popular anti-depressants because they are not addictive and have few side effects. Side effects can include insomnia, nervousness, headaches, dry mouth, and lowered sex drive.

Antidepressants aren't "happy pills," but they do help depression sufferers to feel more positive and think more clearly.

Antidepressants aren't "happy pills," but they do help depression sufferers to feel more positive and think more clearly. One woman described herself as being so paralyzed by her depression that she couldn't make decisions or focus during a traumatic period in her life. An antidepressant didn't take away her pain but it did help her concentrate and make decisions to resolve her problems. If an SSRI doesn't help, there are other drugs that your doctor can try. Some, however, have more serious side effects.

You might also consider some kind of counselling or therapy to accompany your medication. While medication helps greatly, you may still need to deal with what caused your depression in the first place, if, in fact, it has a cause. Learning to deal with your stress or fatigue issues could help prevent a recurrence.

WHAT'S THE ALTERNATIVE?

St. John's wort is a popular herbal antidepressant that has been shown to be as effective as Prozac for mild to moderate depression, although it's not clear yet how it actually works. Don't mix it with other medications without checking first with your doctor. Side effects can include an allergic reaction, upset stomach, dizziness, and sun-sensitivity.

HOW TO BE SUPPORTIVE WHEN YOUR PARTNER IS DEPRESSED

You already know that the mood you each bring to the moment has an effect on your partner. Just living together tends to improve mood. Married men, in particular, suffer less from depression than single men. The same is true, although not to the same degree, for married women. And the kind of support that husbands provide to their wives makes a difference in how the wives recover from depression. In one study of seriously depressed women, the strongest predictor of recovery was the quality of support she received from her spouse.

When one of you appears to be depressed, the partner can help by pushing for a professional assessment and being encouraging about treatment. Be supportive by being empathetic, hopeful, and positive. Don't try to "snap" the other person out of her low mood or dismiss her feelings of sadness as not a real problem.

Preventing Depression

If you've ever suffered from a depression, you don't want to go there again. Even if you haven't but you're dealing with precursors to depression – stress and fatigue – then you want to find ways to beat back the "black dogs" (as Winston Churchill called his depressive episodes) before they attack.

TAKE GOOD CARE OF YOURSELF

If you don't get enough sleep, eat erratically, and exercise by tapping on a keyboard, you're setting yourself up for a fall. Although it's not proven that fatigue, for example, causes depression, common sense tells you that enough sleep, the right food fuel, and activity will help you stay on an even keel.

We all know people who cut into their sleep, skip meals, and don't exercise so that they can accomplish everything on their list, usually a list of others' needs and wants. Their lists are long because they have partners who don't help enough, kids who live for their ballet and hockey and soccer, bosses who don't understand their other obligations, and parents who need their attention. I've written sympathetically about the difficulties of balancing it all for years. But as I've come back to this issue over and over in the course of writing this book, my sympathy is waning. How much help can one be living in a black funk or, perhaps worse, suffering from a heart condition? Don't get me wrong. If together you're dealing with an illness, deep financial trouble, or some other life crisis, you deserve sympathy and support for the load you're carrying. But if you're two people in a stable relationship without the wolves at the door, you need to rethink priorities to look after yourselves, too. And that's as much our responsibility as all the other responsibilities we're so willing to take on. End of sermon.

SAY NICE THINGS TO YOURSELF

Learn the power of what the experts call positive self-talk. Most of us are unaware of the tape that's running in our head, telling us "You'll never finish the project. Your body is unattractive. Your conversation is uninteresting." When you first tune in to that nasty voice questioning your every move, you may be shocked at the cruel things you think about yourself. But if you decide to, you can change the tape to much more positive messages. "You have an excellent record of finishing on time even when a project has a setback. You have a great smile. Your conversation is warm and engaging."

To change the tape, write down your inner negative thoughts to bring them out into the open. Then beside them, write down your new way of thinking. If your thoughts have become a downward spiral of negativity ("I'll never, I can't, I shouldn't have"), you can take some action: clap your hands and yell "Stop" to break the pattern and reprogram the messages. It's hard work to make yourself so self-aware, but the payoff is huge because you reclaim your energies to get on with your life rather than sabotaging your own efforts.

Be good to each other. Your relationship can be a huge source of strength in managing stress and fatigue and preventing depression. Many studies have attempted to codify how men and women support each other within the relationship, some concluding that men receive more support than they provide to women in the same circumstances. However, a recent study published in *Social Science & Medicine* looked at couples sharing "severely threatening life events" and found that good-quality relationships meant lower rates of depression for both men and women, although the overall rate of depression for women was still higher.

Certainly, having already learned to divvy up work and family responsibilities in a way that feels fair to each of you goes a long way to providing a solid base for dealing with new stresses and responsibilities. And remember the measure of a healthy relationship is the handling of disagreements. Knowing how to fight fair keeps arguments from spinning out of control in a way that sends both your stress meters skyrocketing.

MAKE TIME FOR FRIENDS, FUN, AND ACTIVITY

It's so easy to let friendships and time with extended family slide, especially when you're already pulled in too many directions. But having a network of support is the most important way to prevent depression. It may be hard to believe that picking up the phone and calling your sister will be a deposit in your anti-depression bank but it's true. It's also true that making time for fun – as simple as telling a joke at dinner – will put more deposits in the bank. Finally, losing yourself in an activity – reading, assembling model cars, playing bridge, whatever – allows you to concentrate on something other than worries and lose yourself in the moment.

WALK IT OFF

Exercise has been shown to be as effective in fighting mild depression as Prozac. And it's thought to be effective at keeping depression at bay in the first place.

9

Small Changes

Be honest about how one partner's choice affects
the other and support each other to make
changes. Or you can always just nag.

Small physical reminders like finding a new grey hair, or experiencing a new ache can make each of you acutely aware of your middle-age status. Both of you are equally prone to some changes – you'll both need reading glasses eventually. But men are more likely to get gout, and they may experience joint pain from osteoarthritis earlier than women.

For want of a better organizing device, I've lumped together changes from the neck up, then neck down. From the neck up, here's what to expect may happen to your eyes, ears, teeth and gums, and face. (For changes inside your head, see Exercise Your Mind, page 166.) The section on changes from the neck down deals with the wear-and-tear problems you may experience, like heartburn and back pain, and what you can do to either prevent or treat them.

Some of these changes are inevitable. Others are wake-up calls that a bad habit or poor lifestyle choice is catching up with you. And when a bad habit catches up with one of you, it also catches up with both of you. Take back pain, for example. If you can't get off the couch because of a sore back, then your partner feels restricted, too. And since back trouble can be prevented with exercise, it makes sense for both the sufferer and the partner to make time for that exercise in their daily lives. Be honest about how one partner's choice affects the other and support each other to make changes. Or you can always just nag.

From the Neck Up

EYES

There's no escaping presbyopia. That's the gradual deterioration of your close-up vision; it can begin in your late 30s, is very common by your mid-40s, and is inevitable by your 50s. Your gender doesn't matter, neither does your state of health, your genes, or the colour of your eyes. Presbyopia is the single absolutely unavoidable physical change of midlife – which doesn't mean you won't spend months squinting at the telephone book or "borrowing" your spouse's reading glasses because the light's bad before you accept that presbyopia has indeed happened to *you*.

As the years go by, the crystalline lenses, which are the near-focussing mechanism in your eyes, lose flexibility and can no longer change shape to focus at varying distances. At first you find yourself holding small print at different distances from your eyes trying to focus. Eventually there is no distance that works and you need to correct the problem with glasses or contact lenses.

If you don't have any other vision problems, your optometrist will outfit you with reading glasses to correct the presbyopia. Your eyes will continue to change until you're about 60, so expect to update your prescription every couple of years. You can also try monovision contacts, which involve using one eye for distance and the other eye for close-up. In most people, the brain adjusts; however some people feel dizzy or find their vision is blurry even after the initial adjustment period.

For people who are born both nearsighted and farsighted, there are other solutions:

- ❖ bifocal or multifocal glasses
- ❖ reading glasses worn over contacts
- ❖ bifocal contacts (The quality has improved in the last few

years, and most users are pleased with the results. However, close-up vision is not as sharp as with glasses.).

You may also want to explore the new laser surgery options. At present there is no surgical technique that corrects presbyopia although there is one in clinical trials. However, surgically correcting your nearsightedness or farsightedness may mean you need only a pair of simple reading glasses to correct presbyopia, instead of bifocals.

There are two laser surgery procedures available to correct the cornea. Photorefractive keratectomy (PRK) involves reshaping the surface of the cornea with a laser and is appropriate for low to medium corrections of both nearsightedness and farsightedness. Laser-assisted in-situ keratomileusis (LASIK) is a more invasive procedure that involves creating a tiny flap on the cornea, reshaping underneath, and replacing the flap. LASIK is appropriate for all prescriptions. Both procedures take less than fifteen minutes and cost between $2,000 and $3,000 per eye.

Other Eye Disorders
Presbyopia has the benefit of making you visit your optometrist regularly, which is important for discovering other eye disorders and illnesses that become increasingly common in midlife. Diabetes, hypertension, and multiple sclerosis can be detected by looking at the eyes. No matter how good your vision is, be sure to have yearly eye exams after 40. It's easy to overlook this appointment; so try scheduling back-to-back appointments for the two of you and tying them to another event – a joint Christmas shopping trip, for example. All of the following eye disorders will be checked for during a routine eye exam.

Age-related macular degeneration – Central vision decreases because of deterioration of the macula located near the centre of the retina. The condition can affect both eyes. Symptoms include blurring in the centre of vision with clarity around the edges. Early detection is important; laser treatment may slow your loss of vision although it cannot restore it.

Glaucoma – The disease is characterized by an increase in pressure within the eye itself, called intraocular pressure (IOP), caused by faulty drainage. The pressure builds, usually very gradually, and eventually damages the optic nerve; in about 10 per cent of cases, onset can be sudden. Peripheral vision is affected first, but the deterioration may go unnoticed. Glaucoma, if untreated, can eventually lead to total blindness. Age is a risk factor, and you're at increased risk for glaucoma if you have a relative with the disease, are diabetic, have high blood pressure, or are very near-sighted. Early detection is crucial to halting the deterioration; loss that has already occurred is permanent. Glaucoma affects 1 in 100 Canadians over age 40. Treatment includes eyedrops and medications to decrease IOP. In some cases, laser therapy and surgery may help.

Cataracts – Possible as early as age 40 but most common after age 60, cataracts cause clouding of the lens of the eye. Blurred vision or double vision may also be a sign of a cataract. At one time, cataracts were left untreated until they were "ripe." Now, however, cataracts are removed whenever the sufferer decides the time is right. In a surgical procedure, the cataracts are removed, and in about 95 per cent of cases, plastic lens implants are then inserted in the eye, restoring clear vision.

EARS

What was that? Your electric razor whined close to your ears for five minutes this morning. You spent your day at the plant, working on machinery that grinds, rumbles, squeals, but never stops. After dinner, you fired up the lawn mower and cut the grass. And when your wife whispered, "Good night, sweetie" to you in bed, you didn't catch it and wondered why she rolled over in a huff.

Hearing loss usually begins in middle age; half of us have some loss by age 60. Age-related hearing loss, called presbycusis, describes the ear mechanisms that have changed over the years; for example, the eardrum has stiffened so that it doesn't vibrate as well. But the main cause of hearing loss is not age but too much noise. Noise-induced hearing loss is the result of prolonged exposure to noise or music that's louder than 85 decibels.

HOW LOUD IS LOUD?

Common Sounds	Noise Level in Decibels (dB)	Effect
Jet engine (near)	140	Rapid, irreparable damage in some ears
Shotgun firing Jet takeoff within 30–60 m (100–200 ft.)	130	Threshold of pain (about 125 dB)
Thunderclap (near) Discotheque	120	Threshold of sensation
Power saw Pneumatic drill Rock music band	110	Regular exposure of more than 1 minute can cause permanent hearing loss
Garbage truck	100	No more than 15 minutes unprotected exposure recommended
The average portable cassette player set above the halfway mark on volume control	Decibel level varies	Are you setting your volume too high? Don't play auditory suicide.

continued

Common Sounds	Noise Level in Decibels (dB)	Effect
Subway Motorcycle Lawn mower	90	Very annoying
Electric razor Many industrial workplaces	85	Level at which hearing damage begins if exposure lasts 8 hours
Average city traffic noise	80	Annoying, interferes with conversation
Vacuum cleaner Hair dryer Inside a car	70	Intrusive, interferes with telephone conversation
Normal conversation	60	
Quiet office Air conditioner	50	Comfortable
Whisper	30	Very quiet
Normal breathing	10	Just audible

Source: The Canadian Hearing Society. Reprinted with permission.

The amount of hearing loss you incur depends on how long you are exposed to noise over 85 dB. And for every decibel above 85 that you are exposed to, the faster the hearing loss occurs. According to audiologist Marshall Chasin, coordinator of research at The Canadian Hearing Society, for every 3 dB increase in noise exposure, the damage doubles. So exposure to 85 dB for forty hours a week is the same as being exposed to 88 dB for only twenty hours a week.

It's only the loudness of the noise that affects hearing loss, not the kind of noise or the pitch, so Mozart played at full volume is as damaging to your hearing as the roar of a motorcycle or the pounding of a jackhammer. Any loud noise can also cause a temporary hearing loss, called Temporary Threshold Shift (TTS). If you've ever felt that your hearing is duller after a rock concert or car race, you've experienced TTS, which can last several hours before hearing returns to normal. If you're exposed to loud noise over long periods, TTS eventually results in permanent loss.

Chasin suggests this simple test to find out whether your workplace or some activity is so loud that it's damaging your hearing. Before you go in to work, tune your car radio to an all-talk station and set the volume so that you just understand the announcer. After work, turn the radio on without changing the volume and see whether you can hear the conversation. If you can't, you've experienced TTS during your workday and your hearing could be damaged over time.

To reduce your risk of hearing loss, you have to reduce your exposure to loud noise. Think about when you might be exposed. If you're exposed to noise at work, you should use appropriate ear protection like ear plugs or ear muffs there. But when else? If you're a snowmobiler, for example, you will be exposed to its noise during recreational time in the winter. But if you're a snow-mobiler in the winter, a boater in the summer, you love car races, you work in an assembly plant, and you have teenagers who play their Dixie Chicks LOUD, your whole life is noisy. Think about how to protect your hearing wherever you are.

- ❖ Wear ear protectors in a noisy workplace, when using power tools, or when doing noisy hobbies such as hunting, snowmobiling, or woodworking.
- ❖ Wear earplugs at rock concerts. No, it's not a contradiction. You'll still be able to hear the music, but your hearing won't be damaged.
- ❖ Keep the volume control on your Walkman turned below the halfway point.
- ❖ Limit your time in noisy places like bars and dance clubs. If you can't talk comfortably across a table, then consider the noise level damaging.

MOUTH CARE

Good dental hygiene and regular checkups will protect both of you from the major threat to your kissers, gum disease. Gum disease used to be considered a natural result of aging, but now we know it's a natural result of not flossing. Don't feel too guilty. Only about 15 per cent of Canadians floss regularly.

Plaque is the culprit in gum disease. All day and night, this soft sticky substance forms on the surface of your teeth. Plaque is made up of hundreds of different species of bacteria (lovely!) that build up continually until they are whisked away by thorough brushing and flossing. Some of these bacteria are harmful to your teeth and gums, attacking the tissues and causing inflammation. Eventually plaque mineralizes into a hard substance called calculus, or tartar, which is the stuff the dental hygienist scrapes off when she does a cleaning.

It's tartar that causes the beginnings of gum disease. When tartar forms where the gums attach to the teeth, inflammation can occur. You may notice that your gums are a little red and they bleed when you brush them. This is the early stage of the gum disease called gingivitis.

Eventually infection sets. Your gums are puffy and bleeding more often and they may change in colour. You won't necessarily notice any pain. Over time, gum disease can cause deterioration of not only the gums but the underlying support system for the teeth, leading to abscesses, bone loss, and eventually loss of teeth. Advanced gum disease requires several kinds of treatments, including antibiotics and periodontal surgery. However, the best route is prevention. Although some forms of gum disease may be hereditary, most can be prevented with good dental care. According to the Canadian Dental Association, here are five simple steps to prevent gum disease:

1. Brush your teeth twice a day. Take your time and brush gently.
2. Floss your teeth every day. The best time to floss is just before going to bed at night.
3. Check your mouth, teeth and gums regularly for:
   - a change in the colour of your gums
   - gums that are red around your teeth
   - gums that bleed every time you brush or floss
   - bad breath that will not go away
   - a taste of metal in your mouth
   - shiny, puffy, or sore gums
   - teeth that are sensitive for no reason
4. See your dentist on a regular basis.
5. Eat healthy foods. Healthy foods are good for your general health and your dental health.

NIPS AND TUCKS

If you're going to have a procedure to smooth wrinkles or cosmetic surgery to lift your eyelids or suck fat from your cheeks or thighs, you're most likely to do it in midlife. The years between 35 and 50 are prime years for a little trim or correction of what God gave you. Although Canadian figures aren't available, extrapolation from American figures suggests that about 30,000 cosmetic procedures are performed on middle-aged Canadians in a year. More than 80 per cent of patients are women, although a poll of Canadian plastic surgeons revealed that most had more male patients than they did three years ago.

Banishing Wrinkles

Less invasive, less expensive, and less painful than cosmetic surgery are several minor procedures to plump up or remove wrinkles. Botox injections involve injecting the botulism toxin into the face to paralyze underlying muscles. The paralysis stops the skin from creasing so that your perpetual frown is eliminated. It sounds bizarre, but it has become quite popular. It's not permanent, however, and must be repeated every few months. Other injectables include microfat transplantation, a process in which fat from one part of the body is injected into the area to be plumped up, which smooths the wrinkles. Because the injection involves the patient's own tissue, there's no danger of reaction or allergy. However, it does involve a small incision on the thigh or abdomen to remove the fat for injection.

There are various laser procedures that remove the top layer of skin to eliminate discoloration, unevenness, blemishes, and fine wrinkles. Recovery time is about five days.

The Top Three for Over-35s

Here are the most popular cosmetic procedures performed. All involve some pain and risk of complications.

Liposuction – The most popular procedure, liposuction involves the removal of fat deposits on the cheeks, chin, neck, breasts, fatty areas over the armpits, the trunk, hip areas, buttocks, inner thighs, knees, calves, ankles, and sometimes the arms. What liposuction doesn't do is reduce weight or improve cellulite. The surgeon inserts a tool, called a cannula, underneath the skin through one or more small incisions to suction out the deep fatty tissue. The surgery can be performed either with a local anesthetic, local with intravenous sedative, or a general anesthetic. In some cases, an elastic garment like a girdle must be worn for a period of time after the surgery. Swelling and bruising may take up to eight weeks to disappear.

Eyelid surgery – This operation removes excess eyelid skin and bags under the eyes. On the upper lid, the incision is made along the folds of the lid and excess skin is removed. On the lower lid, the incision is made under the eyelashes and fat deposits are removed. Scars are hidden within skin folds. This surgical procedure is usually performed on an outpatient basis with a local anesthetic or, occasionally, with a general anesthetic. Swelling and bruising may take two weeks to disappear.

Face-lift – Most often, an incision is made starting at the temple, running down along the crease at the front of the ear and then back up behind the earlobe and along the hair line. The skin is lifted from the underlying tissue and repositioned; excess skin is removed and fat deposits are suctioned out. The surgery is performed under general anesthetic and the hospital stay is usually less than 24 hours. Bruising and swelling disappear within three weeks. The skin takes several months to recover its suppleness.

GREY HAIR

Most of us have some grey by our mid-30s, and by 50, half of us are half grey. But you'd never know it by looking around at a group of middle-aged couples. The guys are grey, all right, but the women, for the most part, are not. Most women refuse to accept the inevitability of grey hair, preferring to fork out cash to either stay the colour they remember or try something else – anything else but grey. Men are more likely to accept their grey. Or they may just feel that they have no choice. As a society, we've suspended disbelief to allow middle-aged women a rainbow of possible hair colours, but with middle-aged guys, a dye job doesn't go unnoticed.

Grey hair is the result of lack of pigment. Hair strands contain melanin, a pigment that gives them their colour. At some point, usually genetically determined, melanin is no longer produced

Talking about... hair loss

David, 37, a financial planner, and Sandra, 37, a homemaker, have been married fourteen years. They live in Vancouver, British Columbia. They have three children, ages 8, 10, and 12.

David: Going bald was something I didn't notice at first. Then I did. I thought, Oh my God, why didn't someone tell me? I couldn't stand to wait for it to happen so I decided to meet it half way. I shaved my head.

Sandra: The baldness didn't bother me in the least. It was just his forehead. I'd prefer him to let his hair grow back.

and new hairs grow in colourless or white. You can have a sprinkling of grey hairs for years, then they may appear at a more rapid rate. Usually it's the hair on your head that goes first, although men can sometimes find a grey hair in their beards before they find any on their heads. Eventually, all your body hair gets involved. You know you're really middle-aged when you start comparing with your partner who has more grey pubic hairs.

Going grey is, in rare cases, linked to a glandular disorder, but it's not linked to stress or to getting a terrible shock. And you can't affect the rate at which grey hair comes in by plucking it out or keeping your hair short. Greyness will progress inexorably until your head is covered, unfortunately.

GOING BALD ISN'T FUNNY

"How would you like it?" was how one middle-aged male friend put it when I made a dismissive remark about men who worry about baldness. Come to think of it, I wouldn't like it a bit. And certainly I know that women also find baldness difficult to deal with.

There's certainly a double standard around baldness. Men are expected to shrug it off as a trivial change that comes with aging, whereas for women, baldness is a terrible loss. This partly reflects our double standards about men's and women's appearances, with men having more leeway than women in what's attractive. But the double standard also reflects our callousness toward a change that, for many men, is a huge adjustment that alters their sense of self and is tough on their confidence. For some men, going bald *is* the midlife crisis, and their partners need to be empathetic about the change.

Many conditions can cause hair loss, but the most common is pattern hair loss, or androgenetic alopecia. Both men and women experience pattern hair loss, but men generally experience much greater loss and women aren't as likely to notice changes until after menopause. Men tend to lose their hair in a pattern that starts with loss at the front hairline or at the top back of the head (the bald spot) and advances over the top. Women tend not to develop bald spots but rather lose hair over the entire head, causing an overall thinning.

Pattern hair loss, inherited from either parent, is related to hormone levels in the blood. In men, androgens, in particular testosterone, circulate in the blood and are converted by an enzyme into another form of testosterone called dihydrotestostorone, or DHT. It's DHT that triggers hair follicles to begin producing less hair. It's not that hair loss is accelerated but rather that new hairs are not growing in at an appropriate rate to replace old ones. Also, the hairs that do grow in are thinner, lighter, and shorter. By age 30, one-third of men have some balding; by age 50, about half of men are bald. In women who have a genetic predisposition to pattern hair loss, estrogen in their blood protects them from the condition until after menopause. At menopause, they may begin to experience thinning hair.

The connection to testosterone has led some people to believe that baldness is actually related to higher testosterone levels. Unfortunately, for men who saw this as a small consolation for going bald, even this isn't true. It's the hair follicle's receptiveness to DHT that makes the difference. Even on the same head, some follicles are programmed to keep growing while others are not.

What to Do?
Four main treatments are available:

Finasteride (Proscar) – Although not a cure for baldness (there isn't one), this medication, taken once daily, slows the conversion of testosterone into DHT, allowing hair to continue growing. This medication can cause fetal defects in male babies, so it cannot be taken by women who are or may become pregnant. It also has numerous other side effects and results are not permanent. It is only effective while it is being taken.

Minoxidil (Rogaine) – This medication is rubbed directly on the scalp twice a day. It has been shown to slow hair loss in some patients and to stimulate new growth in a small number. Some reports suggest it is more effective in women than in men. Results are not permanent. It is only effective while it is being used.

Hormone Replacement Therapy – For women experiencing hair loss after menopause, HRT may maintain hair growth.

Follicular transplants – Hair transplantation has come a long way from the days when the patient's scalp looked like a doll's head. The process of strip harvesting has made the difference. Narrow strips of skin from the back of the scalp are removed, leaving virtually no scarring. From these strips, minigrafts of two to three hair roots or micrografts of one hair root are separated and implanted into tiny incisions in the thinning or bald areas.

Scalp reduction – This process involves a series of surgical procedures to reduce the bald spot. This may be followed by follicular transplants in any remaining bald area.

From the Neck Down

ACHES AND PAINS

Creaky knees. A sore back. Gout, of all things. And, let's not forget heartburn. The possibility of more aches and pains comes with the territory of midlife. Most of them are "wear and tear" problems. Joint cartilage starts to wear. Spinal discs can't take the pressure and swell. And in the case of heartburn, it's the sphincter between the stomach and the esophagus that no longer closes properly.

Aches and pains make us feel old and can make us limit our activity – "Not tonight, dear, I have heartburn." The advice for just about every sign of midlife wear and tear is to treat the problem and then take action to prevent a recurrence.

Back pain – If you haven't already experienced it, you will. Just about everyone in midlife has at least one attack of acute back pain. It is most commonly caused by simple muscular strain, but it can be caused by a worn facet joint in the spine, a bulging or herniated disc, or a muscle spasm. Most back pain goes away with or without treatment in one to two months. Very rarely does back pain require surgical intervention. Rather, the best approach is to treat the acute symptoms and then begin a program of exercise to prevent a recurrence.

If your back hurts, although you may not want to move, you should probably crawl off to your doctor or chiropractor for an

---

Ouch! Keep Moving!

When some part of your body hurts, you naturally want to protect it by staying still. But when it comes to pain caused by wear and tear – back pain, the pain of osteoarthritis – the advice is to be conscientious about exercise, after an initial short period of rest during acute pain. That's because inactivity just weakens the surrounding muscles, making the bad disc or the stiff joint even more open to injury because it has less support.

assessment. He or she may take X-rays to rule out any serious dis-order and to diagnose your particular point of weakness.

People with back pain used to take to their beds but now the advice is to limit bed rest to as few days as possible and no more than five days. Otherwise your muscles just become weaker and you can get depressed lying there feeling ancient.

Your doctor may prescribe an anti-inflammatory or muscle relaxant. You can also take ASA or acetaminophen. A cold pack may also relieve some pain. Heat isn't recommended for acute back pain because it can cause more inflammation; however, some sufferers find it helps them.

Chiropractic manipulation of the spinal vertebrae may help ease pain more quickly. In surveys, chiropractic is the treatment most back pain sufferers prefer. Massage can also help.

Once the pain has eased, it's time to start stretching and strengthening those back and abdominal muscles to support your spine and improve your posture. Regular walking is also good for your back. And remind yourself of the proper ways to lift so that you avoid back strain at all times. And finally, consider whether your weight affects your back strength. The combination of extra weight and poor abs is not good for what ails you.

OSTEOARTHRITIS

A sore joint or stiffness, particularly in the morning, may be an indication of osteoarthritis. The joints most commonly affected are in the hips, knees, feet, and spine. Osteoarthritis is age-related. Most of us won't feel it until after age 40, unless we've been line-backers or rugby players whose joints have taken more than their fair share of pounding. In their 40s, more men than women have the problem, particularly men in heavy manual work such as min-ing or construction, which can be tough on joints. After age 60,

Talking about . . . staying physically active

Ron, 40, a heavy-equipment mechanic, and Martha, 39, a sign painter, have been married twenty years. They live in Wingham, Ontario. They have two children, ages 9 and 12.

Ron: I just turned 40. I'm worried about the changes that will slow me down a little bit. I'm on my feet all day and it's a demanding job. I don't play hockey anymore because it bothers my back and I need my energy at work. I go hunting and you have to be able to walk ten or fifteen miles a day. I know that in later years, I won't be able to do that.

Martha: I have a physically demanding job as well, and I don't know how much longer I can do it. So there might be a career change for me.

osteoarthritis is an equal opportunity condition, affecting both men and women.

Picture a joint, with two bones held together by ligaments and tendons and with a cushion of cartilage in between. Overuse and injury can wear out the cartilage to the point that the two bones eventually touch and rub together. There aren't any nerve endings for pain in cartilage, but there are in bones, ligaments, tendons, and the surrounding muscles, which is where the pain of osteoarthritis comes from.

You may feel pain in a joint after some activity or after long periods of inaction. If the pain comes from overuse, you need to rest the joint to relieve the pain. But it's also important to continue using the joint and exercising the surrounding muscles to keep the joint limber and supported by strong musculature.

Osteoarthritis starts off slowly, causing minor aching, and then gradually progresses. Don't decide to be stoical and ignore it until it causes you major distress. While no treatment can stop or reverse the disease, your doctor can help you manage it with pain relief, anti-inflammatories, and exercise to slow joint damage. Your doctor may also suggest that you lose weight if you're overweight because extra weight can put strain on knee and hip joints. And if you do heavy physical work or play hard at sports, wear whatever protective equipment and padding is appropriate to protect your joints.

GOUT

Gout is a guy's disease. It's been described as men's equivalent to labour pains, except that instead of lasting hours, it can last weeks. More than 80 per cent of gout sufferers are men and they are most likely to have their first attack in their 40s.

Gout, a form of arthritis that attacks joints, occurs from a buildup of uric acid in the body. Uric acid, the waste product of food and drink, is normally excreted in urine. But when not excreted, excess uric acid builds up and collects in the joints where it produces long, sharp crystals that hurt like hell.

A first attack is very often in the joint of the big toe. It gets hot, inflamed, swollen, red, and very painful. An attack may last a few days or as long as three weeks. One guy I know with gout in his big toe said he couldn't stand even the touch of the bed sheet for a few nights until the swelling came down. Other joints can also be affected, including ankles, knees, elbows, and fingers.

Although gout can have a genetic base, it's also linked to excess alcohol consumption and obesity. That doesn't mean that all gout sufferers are wine-swilling, gluttonous Henry VIII look-alikes. But the connection to diet makes gout yet another illness that responds to lifestyle changes.

Some foods, especially high-fat ones, and some alcoholic drinks have high levels of purine, which turns into uric acid in the blood. Avoiding foods high in purines can reduce your risk of experiencing gout attacks.

Foods High in Purines

- anchovies
- beer
- brain
- fish roe
- gravies
- heart
- herring
- kidneys
- liver
- mussels
- sardines
- sweetbreads
- wine
- yeast

Foods That Have Moderate Levels of Purine

*   ❖ dry beans and peas   ❖ seafood
*   ❖ meats   ❖ shellfish
*   ❖ poultry

Attack!

Treat the pain and swelling of a gout attack by taking ibuprofen (not aspirin, which affects how the kidneys can handle uric acid levels), by keeping the joint raised, and by applying ice. Drink lots of water to flush out uric acid. Your doctor can prescribe anti-inflammatories and stronger pain killers. You may want to ask for a prescription to have on hand, in case of another attack.

Prevent further gout attacks by reducing your alcohol consumption and losing weight if you need to but don't go on a rapid weight loss campaign because it can actually aggravate gout. If you have frequent attacks, your doctor may suggest that you take a medication such as allopurinal daily to lower your uric acid levels. Gout is also linked to high blood pressure, so keep your blood pressure in check. Some medications for high blood pressure, such as diuretics, actually increase uric acid levels, so discuss your options with your doctor.

Pseudogout

As if gout isn't nasty enough, it has an impostor sidekick. Pseudogout usually affects both men and women after age 65. It has many of the same symptoms as gout but the cause of the pain is a different crystal, called calcium pyrophosphate.

HEARTBURN

A pizza after the movie sounded good, but now you're sitting up in a chair instead of lying in bed asleep because every time you lie down, heartburn has you by the throat. If you experience heartburn frequently, you have lots of company. About 40 per cent of Canadians suffer from it and have to reach regularly for antacids to quell the pain.

Heartburn comes with middle age, after a few years of not-so-terrific eating habits. Big meals, eating too close to bedtime, fatty and spicy foods, too much coffee and alcohol all take their toll on the digestive system. Heartburn results when the stomach acids rise up past the lower esophageal sphincter (LES) into the esophagus. The acids irritate the esophagus, which causes the discomfort.

Most heartburn sufferers take antacids that neutralize the stomach acid. Or they try the newer medications now available over the counter called H_2 antagonists, or acid blockers. These medications block the effects of histamine-2, a chemical that tells the cells in your stomach to produce acid. Unlike antacids that are taken after heartburn occurs, acid blockers are taken before a meal that might cause heartburn.

Self-medicating is fine for the occasional attack of heartburn, but if you experience symptoms daily or several times a week, or if your symptoms are getting worse, you should see your doctor. Very few heartburn sufferers actually mention the condition to their doctor because they think it's just the expected result from eating spicy food or overeating. But heartburn can lead to more serious esophageal problems, including gastro-esophageal reflux disease (GERD). Over time, these stomach acids can severely damage the esophagus and even predispose some sufferers to esophageal cancer. GERD sufferers may experience chest pain, a cough, and shortness of breath along with their heartburn. New

Prevent Heartburn and Protect Your Esophagus

❖ Eat slowly and chew your food well.

❖ Don't eat big meals.

❖ Give your stomach at least three hours to digest a meal before
lying down or going to bed.

❖ Avoid the food and drink that set you off. These are usually
alcohol, drinks containing caffeine, peppermint, and foods that
are high-fat, acidic, or spicy.

❖ Stop smoking. Smoking increases the buildup of stomach acids
and may relax the LES muscle so that the acid can rise.

❖ Lose weight if you're overweight. Carrying extra weight puts
pressure on the LES muscle so that it doesn't seal properly.

❖ Wear loose, non-restricting clothes.

❖ Prop up your bed so that your head is higher than your stomach,
which helps to reduce the reflux into the esophagus.

❖ Discuss all your medications with your doctor to be sure you're
not taking anything that might make your symptoms worse.

prescription medicines, called proton pump inhibitors, can successfully turn off stomach acid production to allow your esophagus to heal.

Your doctor can help determine if your heartburn signifies
other disorders that should be treated differently. A 1997 international study concluded that about 40 per cent of people with
poor digestion suffered from motility problems. If you have
poor motility, the stomach doesn't move food as quickly as it
should; the food remains in the stomach, causing bloating,

belching, nausea, feeling full quickly, and vomiting. If your problem is motility rather than acidity, your doctor may prescribe a motility agent.

As you move through middle age together, be clear with each other about what changes you need to accept with grace and what changes signal the need to make new lifestyle choices as a couple. If you allow yourselves to fall into the trap of blaming every new ache on age, you miss the fact that you can support each other in your efforts to stay strong and feel terrific.

10

Nasty Diseases

*You're each at risk for different diseases –
prostate cancer and breast cancer being the
obvious examples – and your risk of other
diseases also differs by gender.*

Depending on the point of view, midlife is the time when we first realize our mortality and begin to worry about the possibility of disease. Or, if you believe the MIDMAC researchers, most people in midlife feel pretty darn healthy but may actually underestimate their risk of illness. Either way, some diseases and conditions are more likely with age, although being middle-aged doesn't mean you'll necessarily experience any of them. You're each at risk for different diseases – prostate cancer and breast cancer being the obvious examples – and your risk of other diseases also differs by gender. Heart disease shows up in men much earlier than women; under age 45, arthritis is more common in men than in women. The lifestyle choices you make together can help you both avoid certain diseases, no matter what your individual risk. Here's what you need to know about signs, symptoms, and prevention.

Prostate Trouble

Prostatitis – This condition, in which the prostate becomes inflamed, mostly affects men under the age of 40. Although it can sometimes be caused by a bacterial infection, the majority of cases have no discernible cause. Your doctor will diagnose prostatitis from an analysis of a urine sample containing some semen. Getting the semen into the bladder and, therefore, into the urine involves a prostatic massage through the rectum.

The most easily treated form of prostatitis is acute bacterial prostatitis. It often comes on quickly; symptoms include a burning sensation when urinating, and the sensation of needing to urinate frequently although sometimes unable to pass water. You might also have a fever, or a pain in the lower back or abdomen, and feel generally unwell. Treatment involves a course of antibiotics.

Occasionally, when the infection no longer responds to antibiotics, acute bacterial prostatitis becomes chronic bacterial prostatis. Along with the symptoms of acute prostatitis, you may suffer from pain with ejaculation. Treatment includes repeated regimes of antibiotics. In some cases, the condition recurs as soon as the first prescription of antibiotics is finished.

Nonbacterial prostatitis is a more problematic condition because there is little treatment. Symptoms are the same as for acute bacterial prostatitis, but they don't respond to antibiotics and may linger for weeks or even months. It is not a serious condition, but it can lay you low until it clears up on its own.

Prostatitis in its several forms doesn't affect potency (although painful ejaculation can't be pleasant), and some experts suggest that regular ejaculation may even be beneficial by emptying the prostate gland.

Benign prostatic hyperplasia (BPH) – With age comes a steadily growing prostate gland, although no one is sure why this happens. Most researchers believe there is a link to testosterone levels, but the link is not clear. The prostate enlarges first in puberty, when higher levels of testosterone circulate in the body. Before puberty, a boy's prostate weighs about a gram. After puberty, it weighs about 15 grams, which remains constant until about age 45, when it goes through another growth cycle, even tripling its size. It's described as growing to the size of a lemon or even a grapefruit, from its original walnut size. Not all men are affected by this growth, however. By age 50, about half of men have symptoms as a result of an enlarged prostate; by age 70 about 80 per cent of men do. Since the prostate wraps around the bladder, an enlarged prostate (benign prostatic hyperplasia) can press on the urethra and eventually block urine flow. Or your symptoms may remain mild, causing no major problems.

WHAT TO DO ABOUT AN ENLARGED PROSTATE

An enlarged prostate on its own probably requires no treatment. Occasionally, a swollen prostate can cause complications such as completely blocking urine flow, which requires immediate surgery. However, you can usually wait until the symptoms cause you enough grief before you decide to have something done. Many men never experience symptoms so bothersome that they have to be treated.

Several medications can slow – even reverse – prostate enlargement and alleviate symptoms. Finasteride blocks testosterone's effects on prostate growth. However, its side effects include impotence and a drop in libido. Alphablockers, such as terazosin and prazocin, reduce symptoms by relaxing the muscles in the prostate and bladder. The most common side effect of alphablockers is dizziness.

When medication is no longer enough, you'll need to consider surgery. The most common surgical procedure

Go with the Flow

Do you have any of these signs of an enlarged prostate?

* Urgency to urinate. Once you realize you have to go, you have to go right then!
* Urinating more often.
* Getting up in the night to urinate once or more often.
* Feeling that your bladder hasn't been emptied even after urinating.
* Slower urine flow.
* Urine stream that starts, stops, and dribbles.

Since these signs of an enlarged prostate are also signals of an infection or a more serious condition, such as prostate cancer, don't self-diagnose (I'm 50. I'm dribbling. It's only my prostate). Instead, have your symptoms checked out.

is called transurethral resection of the prostate, or TURP. The surgeon, working up through the urethra, cauterizes the obstructing prostate tissue. Transurethral prostate surgery technology is improving rapidly. Doctors now use lasers, radio waves, and microwaves to destroy the tissue.

Complications of TURP include infection, erection difficulty, incontinence, and sterility. However, improved surgical techniques have decreased the risks of these complications.

Prostate Cancer

Prostate cancer is the most common cancer in men over the age of 50 and the second leading cause (after lung cancer) of cancer deaths. As with other forms of cancer, the older you are the higher your risk. But prostate cancer is deceptive. Most cases are slow growing and can be present in a man's prostate for years without causing symptoms. It's estimated from autopsy research that one in five 50-year-olds has prostate cancer and half of 70-year-olds have it. Yet most will never be affected by the presence of the cancer cells. That's why doctors say, "More men die with prostate cancer than from prostate cancer."

But prostate cancer is a silent killer. Unless it is picked up through a medical test or in a routine checkup, the sufferer may have no sign of its presence. Problems with urinating are easily confused with the symptoms of an enlarged prostate. You may not find the first signs of the cancer until after it has spread to lymph nodes or to the bones, causing pain.

And like breast cancer in women, prostate cancer is greatly feared by men not only because it can ultimately be a killer but because the treatment can seem as bad as the disease, affecting as it does libido, potency, and fertility.

Protecting Your Prostate

Although these suggestions aren't all proven, none can hurt.

❖ Eat right. Low-fat diets are linked to lower levels of prostate cancer. Also, lowering blood cholesterol may reduce symptoms of prostate enlargement. Several studies have linked high intakes of lycopene (found mostly in *cooked* tomatoes), beta-carotene (found in orange and dark green fruits and vegetables), and fibre with lower prostate cancer risk. And now soy is being touted as the food to eat to protect against prostate cancer.

❖ Get off your butt and exercise. Men who are active may be less likely to develop prostate problems than men who are sedentary. Prolonged sitting actually puts pressure on the gland.

❖ Go when you have to go. Urinating when the urge hits rather than waiting avoids stress on the whole urogenital system, which is good news for the prostate.

❖ Avoid spicy foods and alcohol. Both can increase bladder irritation, which can make symptoms of an enlarged prostate worse. However, a recent study published in the *American Journal of Epidemiology* found men who enjoyed moderate alcohol consumption (one to three drinks per day) had a threefold decrease in prostate enlargement. As always, moderation is the key.

❖ Ejaculate frequently. Some researchers say it makes a difference; others say it's an old wives' tale. It certainly can't hurt.

❖ Soak your tush. A warm twenty-minute bath once a week increases blood flow to the pelvic area and may reduce muscle spasms and even prostate swelling.

GETTING CHECKED OUT FOR CANCER

A man in midlife has some difficult choices to make about how to be monitored for prostate cancer. By the time a patient is 50 (or sometimes earlier), doctors may include a digital rectal examination in a routine medical checkup. This sometimes uncomfortable procedure involves a gloved finger inserted into the rectum to palpate the prostate for lumps or nodules. The doctor can feel only part of the prostate in this test, leaving half the possible cancers out of reach. As well, just as a manual breast exam may not detect cell abnormalities, the digital rectal exam can't detect cell changes either. Most cancers detected this way are no longer confined to the prostate but have already spread elsewhere in the body. The Canadian Task Force on Preventive Health Care debated about five years ago whether the test was worth keeping on the list of recommended procedures during a periodic health exam because it has limited success as an early detection test. The task force decided to give the test a C rating, stating that there wasn't enough evidence either for it or against it as part of the checkup. So even if you're having the test done periodically, it's not much of a safeguard for early detection of cancer.

You may be offered the newer prostate specific antigen (PSA) test. PSA is an enzyme produced by prostate cells, and the level of PSA in the blood is considered a measure of prostate disease. As well, the trend of PSA levels is considered important. So if the level changes significantly after several tests that have the same results, your doctor may want to investigate further. The problem with the PSA test is that it has a high rate of false positives, meaning that the test indicates cancer when none exists. On top of that, it doesn't indicate whether the cancer is slow-moving or one of the minority of aggressive cancers. So all PSA can do for you is tell you that you *might* have prostate cancer. It could be a benign cancer that won't ever cause symptoms or affect you in any way. It could be an aggressive cancer that spreads rapidly. Or it could not be a cancer at all.

To find out what it really is, you'll need a more invasive test than the PSA blood test. You may have a transrectal ultrasound of the prostate (which also has a high rate of false positives) as well as one or more prostate biopsies, in which prostate tissue is removed via the rectum or urethra. The Canadian Task Force on Preventive Health concluded that between 67 and 92 per cent of patients with positive PSAs will undergo unnecessary biopsy. And even if it is concluded that you do have prostate cancer, you'll be faced with the decision about whether to pursue treatment immediately or to adopt "watchful waiting" – further testing every few months to determine the rate at which the cancer is growing.

The PSA test is not recommended as part of a periodic checkup, although many doctors offer it and many men want it. It's a difficult choice you need to discuss together. In some ways, the man's dilemma mirrors the dilemma women under the age of 50 face in whether to have routine mammograms. Neither procedure is proven to be useful at saving lives. And once you enter the world of testing, you may find yourself on a spiral of more and more invasive procedures, some of which may do you more harm than good. But then again, as someone who went for her first mammogram at 45, I can understand wanting to give yourself every available chance of catching cancer early. Deciding on the PSA is like many other decisions you're both asked to make about your health in midlife. Nothing is clear-cut. You're always balancing risks. Beyond keeping yourselves informed, you also need good medical support as you go through the decision making.

And take some comfort from the fact that many doctors are

just as frustrated as their patients at the lack of clear knowledge about prostate cancer screening. Dr. Neill A. Iscoe, writing in the *Canadian Medical Association Journal* in December 1998, says that not enough money is being spent on prostate cancer research. "Given the current burden of this disease and the increase that is looming as baby boomers enter the age group in which incidence rates of prostate cancer rise steeply, the time to find answers is now. In the meantime, the best we can do is be honest with our patients about what we know and what we don't know regarding prostate cancer screening."

At least one research centre for prostate cancer got a big infusion of funds in 1999. Multimillionaire businessman Jim Pattison of Vancouver was so impressed with his urologist, Dr. Larry Goldenberg, who heads up the prostate cancer research centre at Vancouver General Hospital, that he gave the world-renowned centre $20 million. In an interview with *The Globe and Mail*, Dr. Goldenberg was understandably effusive: "This is a great day for the men of British Columbia, and a great day for the men of the world," he said.

Hysterectomy

This surgery is so common – 60,000 Canadian women a year have this procedure to remove their uterus – that it deserves its own section, even if it isn't a disease. Hysterectomy has become a controversial procedure in recent years because many women and doctors have questioned whether the operation is performed unnecessarily and whether other procedures would be more appropriate treatment for the problems that hysterectomies are meant to solve. Canada has the second highest rate of hysterectomy operations in the world, after the United States. Whether you'll have a hysterectomy depends very much on where you live in Canada. Women in rural areas are more likely to have hysterectomies than women in urban areas. If you live in Newfoundland you are more likely to have a hysterectomy than if you live in British Columbia. A report by the Ontario Medical Association and the province of Ontario suggests that, at least in Ontario, doctors perform too many hysterectomies because the procedure is more lucrative than non-surgical alternatives. It also suggests that doctors themselves are not aware of all the alternatives.

Most hysterectomies are performed on women in midlife, and the most common reason for the operation is to remove fibroids. Fibroids are non-cancerous tumours that grow on the inside, the outside, and between the layers of the uterus. Many women (estimates are as high as 50 per cent) have fibroids but most women have no problems from them. In other women, fibroids cause pain, heavy menstrual bleeding, long periods, and abdominal bloating. Fibroids may also enlarge to press on other organs.

Other reasons for hysterectomies are heavy menstrual bleeding (hormonal fluctuations in perimenopause can cause this), endometriosis, uterine prolapse, and cancer of the cervix, endometrium, or ovaries. Hysterectomy is a necessary and

What's Involved in a Hysterectomy

A total hysterectomy includes removal of the uterus and cervix; a subtotal hysterectomy leaves the cervix. Radical hysterectomy includes removal of the uterus, cervix, ovaries, and fallopian tubes. In the past, hysterectomies have been performed through an incision in the abdomen, but more recently the uterus is removed through the vagina or by using laparoscopic techniques that require only small incisions. The length of hospital stay and recovery time are much shorter with the newer techniques. Recovery time for an abdominal hysterectomy is about six weeks; for a vaginal or laparoscopic procedure, it's about two weeks.

Talking about . . . recovering from a hysterectomy

Gisele, 40, an administrative assistant, and Pierre, 42, a glass installer, have been married nineteen years. They live in Edmonton, Alberta. They do not have children. Gisele had a hysterectomy to treat endometriosis but neither of them was prepared for the time it took for her to recover.

Gisele: My gynecologist started me on estrogen replacement therapy the day after my hysterectomy. There wasn't any question in my mind that I would take it, but it wasn't helping me. I had hot flashes and mood swings, and I put on weight. At first my gynecologist was very good at explaining to me what [estrogen replacement] options I had. Then after two or three months, I felt she was too busy for me. That really bothered me, so I went looking and I found a family physician who was very helpful.

Pierre: For several years, nothing worked. For a while, we stayed away from each other. She went upstairs, I went downstairs. It was probably the best way. Whenever I'd say something, she'd start crying. I'd think, Here we go again.

Gisele: We're both very independent people, and it seemed the best way for certain times. He was always there to try and encourage me. He tried his best.

Pierre: When she started to lose weight, she started feeling good about herself. Before that, she didn't feel good about herself. I think the biggest problem was that when the doctor told her, six weeks after surgery, to go ahead and start doing her activities again, she just wouldn't go. She was scared to go and that's when she put on all the weight. But now that she's finally got herself back to aerobics, she feels better about herself.

Gisele: It seemed to escalate. I'd put on weight, then because I put on the weight, I'd feel depressed.

Pierre: I would say that in the last six to seven months, things have improved greatly. I think that Gisele thinks she did make the right decision.

Gisele: It's been a long haul. I don't regret my decision [to have a hysterectomy] anymore. Things are starting to fall into place. I was very active before surgery, and now that I'm exercising four times a week, I've lost thirty pounds.

life-saving procedure to remove cancerous growth or when there is life-threatening hemorrhaging. In other situations, a hysterectomy is just one of several choices of treatment for relieving symptoms and you need to compare all options.

For some women a hysterectomy can be a godsend, finally eliminating the pain and discomfort of conditions such as fibroids and improving quality of life. But for other women the surgery brings with it problems that they may not have anticipated. More research is being done on the role of the uterus in woman's continuing health. There is some indication that a woman whose uterus has been removed is more susceptible to illness, such as osteoporosis. Her sexual functioning may be affected, or she may suffer depression.

CHECK OUT YOUR ALTERNATIVES

Not every option is available in every community. If you live in a small community, you may need to ask your doctor for a referral to a larger centre. Consider that the Ontario Medical Association report found that fewer women living near a medical school had hysterectomies than women in other areas.

Medical Therapy

Your doctor may suggest medications such as birth control pills to control heavy menstrual bleeding, or non-steroidal anti-inflammatory drugs such as ibuprofen to reduce flow as well as menstrual pain. Hormone treatments to block estrogen production can reduce pain and bleeding and shrink fibroids. However, the hormone treatments have serious side effects and should be used for only a short period as a temporary relief.

Surgical Therapy

Fibroid embolization – This procedure, which is being studied at several Canadian hospitals, may reduce the number of hysterectomies performed to remove fibroids. Small plastic particles are shot into the uterus through a catheter threaded to the uterus through an artery, from a small incision in the groin. These particles cut off the blood supply to the fibroids causing them to shrink and eventually be sloughed. The uterus remains intact. The treatment requires no general anesthetic and only an overnight hospital stay. However, severe cramping and pelvic pain can occur, so it's best to take a week away from work.

Myomectomy – This abdominal surgery removes the fibroids but not the uterus. It's suitable for the removal of one or two fibroids, but not several fibroids in different parts of the uterus. In about 20 per cent of women who have a myomectomy, the fibroids regrow and more surgery needs to be performed. The surgery, which is more complicated than a hysterectomy, requires you to have a general anesthetic and to take several weeks for recovery.

Hysteroscopic myomectomy – This is an outpatient procedure. The doctor inserts an instrument with electric current through the vagina to excise the fibroids. Not all fibroids are accessible this way.

Endometrial ablation – This is an outpatient procedure. The doctor inserts an instrument through the vagina to cauterize the endometrium or uterine lining to reduce long and heavy periods.

Uterine thermal balloon therapy – A balloon catheter is inserted through the vagina into the uterus and filled with water, which is then heated. The heat causes the uterine lining to peel away. The procedure, done on an outpatient basis, is meant to reduce long and heavy menstrual periods.

Diabetes

Like hypertension and prostate cancer, diabetes is one of those illnesses that can be at work in your body for years before you realize you have it. That's why you should have regular checkups once you hit midlife because diabetes can be discovered through a routine blood test.

In her book *Managing Your Diabetes: The Only Complete Guide to Type II Diabetes for Canadians* (Macmillan Canada, 1998), M. Sara Rosenthal says that by the year 2004, one in four Canadians over age 45 will be diagnosed with Type II diabetes. So what is it? And who gets it? As you're probably aware, there are different kinds of diabetes. Type I diabetes is an autoimmune disease that affects the pancreas so that it can no longer secrete the hormone insulin into the blood stream. This form of diabetes is usually diagnosed in childhood or adolescence, or before age 30. The much more common form of diabetes (90 per cent of cases) is Type II. With Type II diabetes, the pancreas secretes insulin but the body's cells can't accept it; the body becomes insulin-resistant. Without insulin, blood sugar (glucose) can't penetrate the cells and provide the energy you need to live. The result is that blood sugar builds up in the blood with nowhere to go. This high level of blood sugar damages arteries, which is why diabetes is associated with heart disease and stroke.

Although you can't get Type II diabetes if you don't have a

Are You at Risk for Type II Diabetes?

You are if you:

❖ have a family member with diabetes.

❖ are overweight.

❖ are sedentary.

❖ are over 45.

❖ have impaired glucose intolerance.

❖ had diabetes during pregnancy.

❖ gave birth to a baby over nine pounds.

❖ are of aboriginal, black, West Indian, or Hispanic descent.

genetic predisposition, getting it is also linked to lifestyle factors, such as being obese and sedentary, and eating a high-fat diet. Your risk increases with age (most cases are diagnosed after 40), and you are more at risk for diabetes if you have a family history of the disease. You can't do anything about your genetic predisposition, your age, or your family history, but you can lower your risk of diabetes by keeping to your ideal weight (losing even three to five kilograms [five to ten pounds] has been shown to make a difference), exercising, and eating a low-fat, high-fibre diet.

Although many people have diabetes without experiencing any symptoms, there are some symptoms you can watch for. If you have just one of these symptoms, you should check with your doctor:

❖ increased appetite and weight gain
❖ unusual thirst
❖ frequent urination, even during the night
❖ excessive fatigue
❖ unexplained weight loss
❖ blurred vision
❖ irritability
❖ itchy skin
❖ slow healing of cuts and sores, or skin infections
❖ tingling or numbness in hands or feet
❖ in women, recurrent vaginal yeast infections
❖ infections that don't heal.

The key to preventing diabetes complications is to catch the disease early.

Diabetes is diagnosed by testing for excessive sugar in your blood. A blood sugar test is done in the morning after you have fasted overnight. Normal blood sugar is in the range of 4 to 6 millimoles per litre. A fasting level higher than 7 indicates you may have diabetes. If your level is only slightly higher, a blood test can be done two hours after meals to confirm. A result equal to or higher than 11.1 on this second test means you have diabetes.

Diabetes comes with serious complications. For men with diabetes, their risk of suffering a heart attack is tripled; for women, the risk increases five times. Diabetes also increases the risk of kidney disease, is a leading cause of adult blindness, and can lead to circulation problems that may require amputation of toes, feet, and lower legs.

Once diagnosed, the treatment focusses on keeping blood sugar levels within the right limits using diet, exercise, and medication. About one-third of people with Type II diabetes can control their illness with lifestyle changes, another third need pills along with lifestyle changes, and the rest need lifestyle changes and daily insulin injections.

When you are diagnosed with diabetes, your world can turn upside down with new diet rules, meal schedules, special foot care, and gadgets like blood glucose monitors. Luckily, there is a strong support network of professionals to help you and your partner through the process. Together you may want to see a dietitian and attend a diabetes education centre.

Heart Disease

Heart disease is high on men's list of worries while women tend to focus their fears on the spectre of breast cancer. But cardiovascular disease is the number one cause of death for both men and women in Canada. If you're a woman, you're eight times more likely to die of heart disease than of breast cancer. For men, heart disease is the cause of one-third of all deaths. If you're a cynic like me when you hear those numbers, you think, We all have to die of something. Which is true. But many of those deaths could have been prevented or, let's be realistic, many lives could have been extended with different lifestyle choices. How you choose to live in midlife determines in large measure how energetic and active the two of you are going to be in old age and, in a few cases, whether you'll make it to old age. And your lifestyle is particularly important in determining whether heart disease will rear its ugly head in your life sooner rather than later.

Your gender is a factor in your experience of heart health and heart disease. Men are at risk for heart disease much earlier in life than women are. For men, signs of heart disease can begin in their 40s. For women, they are more likely to begin in the 50s. Neither sex is immune, although for a long time, women were thought to be. Considering what a killer the disease is, it's hard to understand the confusion. But early research on heart disease conducted in the 1950s and 1960s, although it looked at both men and women, included mostly women who were too young for heart disease. We now know that women are protected by estrogen in their systems until menopause. After menopause, their risk of heart disease increases until age 75, when men and women have the same risk.

Men and women display different symptoms of heart disease as well. Women are more likely to experience angina, the chest pain or tightness (sometimes described as heaviness) that accompanies coronary artery disease. Men's signs of heart attack are more likely to be dramatic, a crushing chest pain, for example. Women's signs are vague and easily confused with other illnesses: neck and shoulder pain, nausea, shortness of breath. Know the symptoms most common for your gender and for your partner's. However, these are generalities, so don't dismiss any possible symptoms of heart attack based on gender. What's important to understand is that you both have a risk of heart disease, with a ten-year difference in possible onset, so making lifestyle changes to benefit your heart will work for both of you, not just one of you.

UNDERSTAND YOUR HEART

Here's a primer on how the heart works and what can go wrong. The heart is a small, hollow pump (about the size of your fist) that beats about 100,000 times a day with enough strength to circulate blood throughout the body right down to your toes. Each side of the heart has two chambers – the right atrium, the right ventricle, the left atrium, and the left ventricle – which are connected by valves that allow blood to flow in one direction only. Like all organs, the heart needs a steady supply of oxygen to do its work. Oxygen and nutrients are what is supplied to the heart by the coronary arteries, which run from the aorta round the outside of the heart to the heart itself.

Atherosclerosis
The entire cardiovascular systems depends on a smooth flow of blood through the arteries to internal organs and back to the heart. But arteries can become narrowed or obstructed with fatty deposits, or plaque. When this substance narrows or even blocks arteries anywhere in the body, it's called atherosclerosis.

Coronary Artery Disease (CAD)
If plaque collects in the coronary arteries, you have coronary artery disease (CAD). Angina is a common symptom of CAD. When oxygen needs exceed the heart's oxygen supply, people experience angina. In men, angina can feel like pressure or tightness in the chest that may spread to the neck, jaw, or arms. In women, it manifests itself in less specific ways and is easily misdiagnosed. Stable angina is brought on in a predictable way: exer-

tion, stress, exposure to cold. It is relieved by rest and medication. Unstable angina doesn't show a pattern, and activities that didn't previously cause angina may begin to cause it. Unstable angina requires immediate medical attention.

Heart Attack

Heart attack is caused by an injury to the heart that occurs when oxygen is cut off. Coronary artery disease is the main cause of heart attack, either because a coronary artery or any artery becomes so clogged that oxygen-carrying blood can't reach the heart, or because a piece of atherosclerotic plaque triggers blood clots that bind with plaque and block the artery. When oxygen is blocked to the heart, the heart muscle is damaged or even destroyed, although if the damage is minor it may recover fully. The difference between angina and heart attack is that angina does not destroy heart muscle but a heart attack may do so.

The key to surviving a heart attack and minimizing heart muscle damage is prompt medical attention. Clot-busting drugs can make the difference between life and death and the difference between a severely damaged heart and one with little or no permanent damage. These drugs must be administered within six hours of an attack. Since a heart attack can mimic other less serious conditions, even heartburn, don't self-diagnose. Go to your emergency department and let the professionals with the fancy equipment decide what's going on. That's what they're there for.

Warning Signs of a Heart Attack

According to the Heart and Stroke Foundation, here's what to watch for.

In the chest:
* mild ache
* heavy, full, or tight feeling

* pressure, squeezing, or burning
* awful crushing pain
* pain that starts in the middle of the chest and spreads to the neck, jaw, or shoulders

Other symptoms:
* odd pain that goes down one or both arms
* shortness of breath, pale, sweating, weak
* sick feeling, throwing up, heartburn
* feeling very nervous or afraid, not wanting to believe it could be a heart attack

What to Do if You Think It's a Heart Attack

* Play it safe – don't wait.
* Tell somebody.
* Dial 911 or your local emergency services number.
* Have someone take you to the hospital right away.
* Call a doctor if your area does not have an emergency services number and the hospital is far away.

Stroke

A stroke is a brain injury caused when the blood supply to the brain is interrupted. Less frequently, the injury is caused by a hemorrhage or bleeding in the brain. Without the oxygen that carries blood to the brain, the brain cells die, leading to disability or death. The brain's blood supply can be cut off by a blood clot in a vein or an artery leading to the brain. Getting immediate medical attention improves your chances of survival and of a full recovery.

According to the Heart and Stroke Foundation, the warning signs of stroke are:

* sudden weakness, numbness, or tingling of the face, arm, or leg
* temporary difficulty or loss of speech, or trouble understanding speech
* sudden loss of vision, particularly in one eye, or double vision
* sudden, severe, unusual headaches or a change in the pattern of headaches
* dizziness, unsteadiness, or sudden falls, especially with any of the above signs.

SO HOW DO YOU MINIMIZE YOUR RISK?

You know the drill – live smoke-free, eat a healthy diet, get regular exercise, drink alcohol in moderation, and lower your stress levels. Check out other sections of this book for the best way to accomplish these choices. Here's the medical evidence for how each of these lifestyle choices benefits your heart.

Living Smoke-Free

Your heart will thank you because, by quitting smoking, you increase the amount of oxygen it receives with every breath. Smoking also raises the levels of "bad" LDL cholesterol and lowers "good" HDL cholesterol. Your risk of heart disease is cut in half within one year of quitting. Within two years, most of the increased risk is eliminated. Women who smoke face an increased risk of cardiovascular disease; they also reach menopause one to two years earlier than women who don't smoke. Once women reach menopause, they lose their heart-protecting estrogen, which puts them at even earlier risk for heart disease. And your partner's heart will benefit when you quit smoking because he or she won't be breathing your second-hand smoke.

Eating Well

Eating high-nutrient, high-fibre, and lower-fat foods will increase your levels of "good" HDL cholesterol and decrease "bad" LDL cholesterol in your blood. In particular, avoid eating highly saturated animal fat and trans fats created in the manufacturing process and found in baked goods and convenience foods. Soy is a food that might lower cholesterol levels. But contrary to what you may think, most of us don't need to worry about the amount of cholesterol in our food. Dietary cholesterol contributes very little to the amount of cholesterol in our body, most of which is manufactured in the liver.

Get Regular Exercise

Exercise helps you maintain an appropriate weight, strengthens the heart muscle (if you exercise within the appropriate heart rate range), and raises the levels of "good" HDL cholesterol.

Lower Stress Levels

Many studies show that higher stress levels, feelings of hostility, anger, or anxiety can raise blood pressure, increase "bad" LDL cholesterol levels, and decrease "good" HDL cholesterol levels. Remember that each of you may have different stress triggers even if your lives have similar family-work patterns. For men, their work is the source of most of their stress, and for women, the stress is more likely centred on family life. Since stress can be "contagious," lowering your own stress level will have a positive effect on your partner as well.

Drink Alcohol in Moderation
Heavy alcohol use raises blood pressure, which raises the risk of cardiovascular disease. But moderate use (no more than two drinks a day) is associated in the research with a lower risk of disease than if you don't drink at all.

Lower Blood Cholesterol
If you've just recently joined the ranks of the middle-aged, you may still be a bit confused about cholesterol testing and what the numbers mean. If you've been middle-aged for a while, you may be an old hand at comparing millimoles with your partner. And you're probably aware that cholesterol testing and medicating to lower cholesterol are both controversial.

First of All, Testing: Who Should, Who Shouldn't
Most health organizations and individual doctors don't recommend cholesterol testing as a general screening tool. But once you reach middle age, it makes sense to be tested at regular intervals, for example, once every five years. And if you have any risk factors for heart disease (you're a smoker, have high blood pressure, or you're inactive), then you may want to be tested every year. A cholesterol test is done on blood taken after you've fasted overnight for twelve to fourteen hours.

Understanding the Results
Cholesterol occurs naturally in the body and is important in some hormone production and cell formation. But too much cholesterol or the wrong ratio of cholesterol in the blood can narrow arteries and cause atherosclerosis. Your doctor will check your "good" HDL cholesterol level, your "bad" LDL cholesterol level, and look at the ratio between the two numbers. Having more good cholesterol can offset the effects of bad cholesterol. Your doctor will be most concerned about your LDL cholesterol level

What Are Your Numbers?

Cholesterol is measured in millimoles per litre. Here's what the
numbers mean for those over 30, according to the Heart and Stroke
Foundation of Canada.

Healthy range: Total cholesterol less than 5.2 mmol/L

Diet changes are recommended if your test reveals any of the
following:

Total cholesterol between 5.2 and 6.2 mmol/L

LDL cholesterol greater than 3.4 mmol/L

HDL cholesterol less than 0.9 mmol/L

Triglycerides greater than 2.3 mmol/L

Dietary therapy is essential, and if not successful, drug therapy may be
necessary when:

Total cholesterol is greater than 6.2 mmol/L

because too much LDL cholesterol increases your risk of coronary
heart disease. And if you already suffer from heart disease or have
had a heart attack, lowering your LDL levels is even more beneficial. Your doctor will also measure your triglycerides, which are
fatty deposits in the blood, because high levels of triglycerides
increase your heart disease risk.

What to Do about High Cholesterol – Drugs or Not?
To reduce LDL cholesterol levels, you should first make changes to
reduce fat in your diet and increase your exercise. However, if you

already have coronary heart disease or you have not achieved a change in your cholesterol levels after several months of trying, your doctor may suggest you try a cholesterol-lowering drug. Several recent studies have shown that drugs can reduce the number of heart attacks suffered by people with high cholesterol. However, you may need to take drugs for many years, even indefinitely.

Lower High Blood Pressure

Most of us have had our blood pressure taken for years. Before age 55, you should have your blood pressure taken at least every two to three years, and yearly after age 55. Your doctor takes your blood pressure using a sphygmomanometer to check both the systolic and diastolic pressure. Systolic pressure is the pressure exerted when your heart contracts, and diastolic pressure is the pressure exerted when your heart relaxes.

$$\frac{120 \; \textit{systolic} \text{ (pressure when heart contracts)}}{80 \; \textit{diastolic} \text{ (pressure when heart relaxes)}}$$

The pressure at which blood flows through the body fluctuates often depending on such things as your activity level, your stress level, and whether you have just had a coffee (caffeine increases blood pressure). But after the activity or once you've calmed down from the fight with your boss, your blood pressure returns to its base line. Normal blood pressure ranges from 100/60 to 130/80 millimetres of mercury (mm Hg) with the average being 120/80. Blood pressure of more than 140/90 indicates hypertension, or high blood pressure. About 10 per cent of the population has high blood pressure.

It's easy to be unaware of small elevations in blood pressure because you're not likely to feel any effects from them. That is the reason hypertension is one of the "silent killers." Too much pressure in the system will, over time, cause damage to your arteries, putting you more at risk for heart attack, stroke, and kidney failure.

High blood pressure can be caused by the usual bad lifestyle choices – overweight, too much food, not enough exercise, heavy drinking, smoking, and high stress, but high blood pressure can also occur for no obvious reason. You go to your doctor for a routine checkup and are told your blood pressure is up. Now what? First you and your doctor need to be sure that you really have hypertension. One high blood pressure reading is not a diagnosis. It could be the result of a heavy meal, the traffic jam that held you up on your way to your appointment, or even just the experience of being tested by your doctor – the so-called "white coat syndrome." Three readings at different times are needed to confirm hypertension.

If your hypertension is mild and tests reveal no organ damage as a result, you may be able to lower your numbers by making lifestyle changes. A diagnosis of hypertension is one of those jolts that should encourage both of you to look at what in your lifestyle needs changing. Getting more exercise, losing weight, making better food choices, quitting smoking, cutting down drinking (no more than two drinks daily for women or three drinks for men), lowering stress levels – this is the basic advice. Consider adding more potassium to your diet (bananas are high in potassium) because there is some evidence that insufficient potassium is linked to hypertension. And you may want to limit your salt intake. Not everyone's blood pressure is affected by salt intake, but for people who are, less salt means lower numbers. You'll also want to get your cholesterol levels checked and if they are high, work on lowering those numbers as well.

If, after several months, your blood pressure remains high, you may want to consider medication. It's a tough decision. All high blood pressure medications have some side effects and blood pressure medication usually becomes a lifelong commitment. Your doctor may need to try several different medications before finding one that works well for you. The Canadian Hypertension Society currently recommends diuretics and beta-blockers as the first line of pharmaceutical defence. These older, less expensive drugs have been tested and shown to reduce the risk of both heart attack and stroke. If neither of them works or if they cause uncomfortable side effects, then your doctor will prescribe angiotensin-converting enzyme (ace) inhibitors or calcium channel blockers.

How low your blood pressure should go has become a point of discussion recently. Most doctors had their patients aim for 140/90, but the recent Hypertension Optimal Treatment Study analysis of 19,000 people in twenty-six countries (including Canada) concluded that those who reduced their diastolic reading – the bottom number – to at least 83 were less likely to suffer a heart attack. People who have diabetes along with their hypertension and whose diastolic reading was 80 or less had fewer cardiovascular problems.

Should You Get Your Own Blood Pressure Monitoring Machine?

Doctors and other experts are divided on this topic. Some consider that the machines are tricky to use, aren't always accurate, and may do more harm than good. But others see real benefits in self-monitoring. Being able to take several readings in different situations can establish whether your blood pressure is affected by salt intake or other lifestyle changes, for example. It helps determine whether you have "white-coat" hypertension. You may reach your blood pressure goals more quickly and be more self-reliant in your care.

If you decide to buy a blood pressure monitoring machine, be sure to take it to your next appointment to test it against your doctor's equipment for accuracy and to receive instruction on the

After a Diagnosis

When one of you is diagnosed with a serious illness like heart disease or cancer, it can't help but affect your relationship.

Cancer

A diagnosis of cancer introduces fear into your lives, says Heather Richards, a social worker at the Kingston Regional Cancer Clinic in Kingston, Ontario. The partner who has been diagnosed confronts the prospect of dying and needs to express his thoughts and fears to his partner. How long a person may spend contemplating death before returning to the task of living is individual, Richards says. The partner of someone diagnosed with cancer has other fears to face, especially the fear of being left behind, and needs the chance to express these fears.

Eventually someone living with cancer begins to focus again on the present – how to handle treatment, how to manage pain, and how the family will make it through the disruption caused by the illness. He or she realizes there is much to do and begins to "fight back." At this stage it's the partner who has a more difficult time, feeling helpless to battle the disease.

Even couples with strong communication skills may struggle during the ordeal of diagnosis and treatment. If communication is breaking down, it's time to get professional help, Richards says.

Heart Disease

Following a heart "event," couples experience two levels of emotion, says Monica Parry, clinical nurse specialist/nurse practitioner for cardiac surgery at Kingston General Hospital in Kingston, Ontario: one shared and the other distinct. Together they feel anxiety and fear. The person who has suffered a heart attack may be depressed, angry, and hostile. His or her partner, on the other hand, may feel guilt and revisit lifestyle decisions, feeling responsible for poor choices. ("Maybe I shouldn't have cooked so much high-fat food." "Maybe I should have quit smoking so she would quit, too.") Both feel a tremendous amount of stress. Men experience their first heart event at a younger age than women. Sometimes their wives become overly protective and coddling, which the men may resent. Few couples openly discuss sex. When they do, Parry says, it's often the supporting spouses who have the most fear; they're afraid that resuming sex might kill their partners. It is important to talk about intimacy because a heart event has the potential to come between the partners. She tells them that having sex takes as much stamina as climbing two flights of stairs.

It is important to understand where heart disease fits on the continuum of your general health. Heart disease is a chronic illness with periods of stability, when all seems normal, and periods of instability, including angina, heart attack, and heart surgery. Education and knowledge help put fears in perspective; it's always better for both patient and spouse to learn as much as they can. Patient support groups, such as the eight-week Heart to Heart program developed by the Heart and Stroke Foundation, can make a huge difference in helping patients and their spouses communicate with each other and feel less isolated and more confident about managing the condition.

best use of the machine. Certainly don't use it to replace regular visits to your doctor or to adjust medications without consulting with your doctor. Have your home unit checked with your doctor's equipment every year.

You have a choice of either an aneroid monitor or an electronic monitor. Aneroid monitors are cheaper, but they're more difficult to use. The more popular electronic monitor typically inflates and deflates with the press of a button, and the numbers immediately appear on the screen. Fully automatic units are the most expensive. Monitors that measure finger blood pressure are not recommended because they are not as accurate.

WHAT'S THE ALTERNATIVE?

Several vitamins and other substances have been identified as helping prevent heart disease and stroke. Most of these can come from a balanced diet. Your daily requirements for antioxidant vitamins C and beta-carotene can be easily met by eating fruits and vegetables. Eating cold-water fatty fish, such as salmon, regularly supplies omega-3 fatty acids, which may help reduce blood pressure and triglyceride levels. However, a few supplements may be worth considering for prevention of heart disease, although evidence is not conclusive. Be sure to discuss with your doctor if you take any supplements.

Vitamin E – This antioxidant may lower "bad" LDL cholesterol levels and prevent heart attacks. 100 to 300 IU daily is recommended.

Folic Acid – This vitamin reduces homocysteine levels in the blood. Elevated homocysteine levels have been linked to artery damage, heart attack, and stroke. Since homocysteine testing is expensive and not yet done routinely in Canada, most people don't know their homocysteine levels. Rather than recommend testing, some doctors recommend supplements as a precaution against possible high homocysteine. No more than 1 mg daily is the recommended amount.

ASA – Since acetylsalicylic acid (ASA) reduces clot formation, it reduces the likelihood of heart attack and stroke in men; less research has been done on its effect in women. However, ASA may not be appropriate for people with extremely high blood pressure. One enteric-coated ASA tablet daily is recommended in dosage ranges from 90 to 325 mg daily, with the higher dose more often recommended for stroke prevention.

Cancer

Although your risk of cancer increases with age, your middle years are not high-risk years. Cancer is primarily a disease of the elderly, with almost half of all cancers diagnosed at 70 or older. In midlife as in younger years, preventing cancer in the first place should be your main focus. The Canadian Cancer Society lists seven steps you can take to help protect you against cancer:

1. Choose to be a nonsmoker and avoid secondhand smoke.
2. Choose a variety of lower-fat, high-fibre foods. Maintain a healthy body weight and limit your alcohol intake.
3. Protect yourself and your family from the sun. Practise regular skin examinations and report any changes immediately.
4. For women, schedule regular Pap tests and mammograms. Practise monthly breast self-examination.
5. See your doctor and dentist regularly for checkups.

6. Be aware of changes in your normal state of health. If you discover a lump or a mole that has changed or a sore that won't heal, check with your doctor immediately.
7. At home and at work, follow health and safety instructions when using hazardous materials.

You should also learn the known causes and the early warning signs of the most common cancers.

Lung cancer – Smoking is the primary cause of lung cancer, which is the leading cause of cancer deaths in both men and women. According to the most recent *Canadian Cancer Statistics*, about one-third of cancer deaths in men and almost one-quarter of cancer deaths in women are the result of lung cancer. The incidence of lung cancer and its mortality rates continue to increase rapidly among women, although they are still only about half as high as rates for men. One positive note in this bleak picture is that the incidence of lung cancer for men has been dropping since 1984 as more men have quit smoking. Your risk increases with the length of time you have smoked. Your risk no longer increases once you quit. Often the first sign of lung cancer is a chronic cough. Lung cancer is not easily treated.

Colorectal cancer – The causes of the cancer that affects the colon and rectum aren't known. A low-fat, high-fibre diet with plenty of foods containing vitamins C and E has been recommended to prevent colorectal cancer. Taking the birth control pill may lower women's risk of this disease. Risk factors include a family history of the disease and having an inflammatory bowel disease such as ulcerative colitis. Signs of colorectal cancer mimic other intestinal complaints. Symptoms include a change in bowel habits (diarrhea or constipation), crampy abdominal pain, a persistent desire to move the bowels with little passage of stool, and bleeding from the rectum (such bleeding is most often caused by hemorrhoids but should always be checked). Check out any intestinal changes with your doctor, and after age 50, discuss your screening requirements with him or her.

Skin Cancer – Too much sun exposure is the usual cause of skin cancer, the most common cancer there is. There are three forms of skin cancer – basal cell, squamous cell, and the more serious melanoma, which makes up about 5 per cent of cases. Slip! Slap! Slop! has become the rallying cry of dermatologists and the Canadian Cancer Society, all anxious to lower the incidence. When you go out in the sun, slip on a cover-up, slap on a hat, and slop on the sunscreen. And recent evidence suggests the public education campaign is working. Statistics Canada reported last year that, after years of steady increases, the rate of melanoma stabilized in Canada. Couples can screen each other for this illness by watching each other's backs. Dr. Wolodymyr Medwidsky, an assistant professor of dermatology at the University of Toronto, suggests that partners look at areas of the body that their mates can't see themselves. About 70 per cent of melanoma cases are found by women either on themselves or their spouses. Melanoma in men occurs most commonly on their backs, and in women on the backs of their thighs and their legs.

IN MEN

Prostate Cancer
See Prostate Trouble, page 229.

Testicular Cancer
In midlife, your risk for this disease decreases. Men at highest risk are between the ages of 15 and 35. Still, you should examine

your testicles regularly by gently rolling them between your thumb and fingers. The first sign may be a hard lump or a feeling of heaviness in one testicle. Do not delay seeing your doctor. Testicular cancer treatment has a high success rate and does not necessarily affect sexual health or reproduction.

IN WOMEN

Breast Cancer

Breast cancer is the most common cancer in women, and may occur earlier than other common forms of cancer. The possibility of breast cancer is a major anxiety for most women in midlife, and fear can be heightened by the way the disease is portrayed. We're told that women have a one-in-nine lifetime risk of developing breast cancer. But women need to understand that only 90-year-olds have to worry about that one chance in nine. For anyone younger, the risk is much less. Because the risk increases with age, a 25-year-old has a less than 1 in 1,000 risk, a 50-year-old a 1 in 63 risk, a 75-year-old a 1 in 15 risk, and a 90-year-old a 1 in 9 risk.

Improvements have been made in breast cancer screening and in treatment for the disease, and both show results in the form of slightly fewer cancer deaths. However, the number of breast cancer cases is increasing, possibly due to the improved screening and to the aging population.

Several causes of breast cancer are suspected although not proven. According to the Canadian Cancer Society, the following risk factors have been identified:

1. Age. Breast cancer is more commonly found in women over the age of 50.
2. Previous breast cancer.

3. A strong family history of premenopausal breast cancer. If more than one first-degree relative (mother or sister) has had breast cancer, then there is an increased risk for developing the disease.

4. The biopsy of a lump results in a precancerous finding of "atypical epithelial hyperplasia."

5. Age at first pregnancy. Women who are over 30 when they have their first child run a slightly greater risk of developing breast cancer than women who had children before the age of 25.

6. Menstruation. Onset of menstrual periods before age 12 and the discontinuation during a late menopause have been associated with a slightly increased risk of breast cancer.

7. Diet. Evidence suggests that a high intake of dietary fat may increase your risk of breast cancer.

The use of hormone replacement therapy (HRT) for five years or more is associated with a slight increased risk of breast cancer. Some research has linked alcohol consumption to breast cancer. While several studies have indicated heavy alcohol consumption raises your risk, new research from the Framingham Heart Study, reported in the *American Journal of Epidemiology*, suggests that light consumption of one or two drinks a day does not increase risk.

Breast Screening
Regular breast screening is the best way to catch breast cancer at the earliest stage possible, when treatment has the highest chance of success and can be the least invasive. But breast cancer screening, like screening for prostate cancer, is fraught with controversy. Women are urged to do regular breast self-examination, in spite of the fact that such examinations have not been proved to lower mortality rates. In Canada, mammograms are only recom-

mended for women over age 50, although many organizations and individual women and their doctors feel that younger women should be screened as well. Mammograms can give false positive results, sending women back for more invasive tests that may prove unnecessary. Or they can give false negative results that may instill a false sense of security. All that said, it's the best system we have. So until researchers come up with the equivalent for breast cancer of the highly successful Pap smear screening for cervical cancer, women would be wise to take full advantage of the screening system we have. Unfortunately, many women aren't doing that. Less than half of Canadian women over 50 get their breasts checked regularly.

Regular breast screening involves three steps:

❖ monthly breast self-examination
❖ yearly clinical examination by a health-care professional
❖ mammograms every two years starting at age 50.

Breast Self-Examination (BSE)
Most breast cancers are still found by women themselves. Some recent research based on Canada's National Breast Screening Study showed that women with good self-examination technique found breast cancer at earlier, more curable stages. To get a lesson in doing BSE properly, call the Canadian Cancer Society, branches of the Canadian Breast Cancer Foundation, or your local breast-screening centre. Provincial and territorial screening programs focus on women 50 and older, are designed to detect early cancers through mammograms, and offer clinical breast exams and advice on BSE by a trained nurse examiner. No physician referral is needed. To locate your nearest centre, call the Canadian Cancer Society's Cancer Information Service at 1-888-939-3333.

Good Technique Counts

There are several recognized methods of examining your breasts. Here are two BSE techniques recommended by the Canadian Breast Cancer Foundation. BSE should be done the same time every month, seven to ten days after the start of your period if you're menstruating or at a fixed day each month. With either method, you should include the area between the breast and the armpit because that area also contains breast tissue. Be sure to use your three middle fingers in a rotary motion and feel with your finger pads (not the tips).

By the clock – Pretend your breast is a clock. Start at "12 o'clock," right below the collarbone. Using the flat pads of your fingers, press gently but firmly in small overlapping circles, moving to the nipple. Do the same at each "hour."

Going in circles – Examine each breast in concentric circles, starting at the nipple and working out.

Using either method, examine your breasts in three positions.

1. *In the shower* – Raise one arm. With fingers flat and soapy, touch every part of each breast, gently feeling for a lump or thickening. Use your right hand to examine your left breast and your left hand to examine your right breast.

2. *Lying down* – To balance the breast on the chest, place a towel or pillow under your right shoulder and place your right hand behind your head. Examine your right breast with your left hand. Repeat on the other side.

3. *In the mirror* – Do a visual check of your breasts with your arms at your sides, then raised above your head. Look care-

fully for changes in size, shape, and contour of each breast. Look for puckering, dimpling, or changes in skin texture, colour or rashes. Check for changes in the nipple, such as being pulled in. With one hand on your hip, tense and push your arm forward to make a pocket under the arm and use the same method as when lying down to check this area. Repeat on the other side. With your arm resting on a firm surface, use the same circular motion to examine the underarm and the side area of your rib cage. Repeat on the other side.

Clinical Breast Examination
You can have this done at a provincial or territorial breast screening centre, or your doctor will include the exam in your regular medical checkup.

Mammograms
It's easy to put off having a mammogram. The procedure is uncomfortable, somewhat embarrassing, and nerve-racking. Get over it. Mammograms can be lifesavers. Studies show that regular mammographic screening of women age 50 and over reduces mortality by 30 per cent by catching breast cancer at early, treatable stages. A recent University of Toronto analysis of results from the Canadian National Breast Screening Study showed that the timing of mammograms in menstruating women affects accuracy. There are fewer false negative results – that is, fewer results that show no cancer when, in fact, cancer is present – when mammograms are performed during the first half of the menstrual cycle rather than the second half. During the first half, breasts are less dense, so they can be compressed more easily, which may be why results are better.

Talk to your doctor about when to have your first mammogram. The Canadian Cancer Society continues to recommend starting at age 50, while some American organizations recommend beginning between ages 40 and 49. The Canadian reasoning is that regular mammogram screening has been proven to lower mortality rates for women between 50 and 69, but it hasn't been proven to lower mortality rates for women from 40 to 49. Mammography misses 10 to 15 per cent of breast cancers in all women, but in younger women the numbers are higher because younger women's breasts are denser. Even though the results aren't as accurate for women under 50, younger women who want mammograms can certainly request them.

Cervical Cancer

Here's a wonderful cancer success story, at least in developed countries like Canada, where the Pap test is readily available. Since 1951, death from cervical cancer decreased from 11 per 100,000 to 2.2 per 100,000 population in 1998. In developing countries, where the Pap test is not available to women, cervical cancer is the most common cancer in women. It is found in women who have had multiple sexual partners and who began sexual activities at an early age. This cancer is also linked to smoking and to infection from the human papilloma virus. Regular screening can detect abnormal cells at a pre-cancerous stage, allowing for effective treatment. How often to have a Pap test depends on the Pap smear screening program in your province. Follow your doctor's instructions. It is a misconception, however, to think of cervical cancer as a young woman's disease. The highest occurrence and mortality is for women over 65.

Endometrial Cancer

Rare before menopause, endometrial cancer cannot usually be detected with a Pap test. New research shows that taking the birth control pill reduces the risk of endometrial cancer. The longer you take the pill, the lower your risk and the longer the protective benefits last after you stop taking the pill. The sign of endometrial cancer is unusual bleeding. Don't dismiss bleeding during or after menopause as just part of the transition. Have regular gynecological exams. Your doctor may perform an endometrial biopsy in the office if unusual bleeding occurs.

Ovarian Cancer

Like many cancers, this one is most common after menopause. And unlike other cancers, it is difficult to detect. Again new research shows that taking the birth control pill reduces ovarian cancer risk. The longer you take the pill, the lower your risk and the longer the protective benefits last after you stop taking the pill. There is no effective routine screening test and early warning signs are vague and easily confused with other problems. Early signs include persistent stomach distention, discomfort, gas, abdominal pain, or lower back pain. Women with a family history of ovarian, breast and/or colon cancer are at an increased risk of developing ovarian cancer. Regular gynecological exams and being aware of subtle body changes may help with detection at early stages when treatment is most effective.

Osteoporosis

If you're a guy, do not skip this section. Yes, osteoporosis affects more women than men, but men don't get off scot-free. About one million Canadian women have osteoporosis; so do 400,000 Canadian men. According to the Osteoporosis Society of Canada, about 70 per cent of osteoporotic fractures occur in women and about 30 per cent occur in men. And elderly men are more likely to die after a hip fracture than women. So bone protection should be a goal for both of you.

Osteoporosis is a disease in which bones lose mass or density faster than they rebuild it. As a result, they become porous and susceptible to breaking. Women reach their peak bone mass between the ages of 20 and 25. Men continue to build bone mass until about 30. In general, men have larger bones than women and higher bone density. After age 40, both men and women begin to experience a decrease in bone mass. For women, this drop is accelerated after menopause. A woman can lose between 2 and 5 per cent of her bone mass every year for five to ten years after menopause.

Osteoporosis is another disease in which damage can occur long before you're ever aware of any physical changes. It also has no cure, although new treatments can slow the deterioration. That's why prevention and early detection are important. You can help prevent osteoporosis by knowing what the risk factors are so that you can minimize your own personal risk. According to the Osteoporosis Society of Canada, those most at risk:

- ❖ are female.
- ❖ are age 50 or older.
- ❖ are past menopause.
- ❖ have prolonged sex hormone deficiencies (decreased estrogen levels in women and decreased testosterone levels in men).
- ❖ had ovaries removed or experienced menopause before age 45.
- ❖ do not get enough calcium in their diet.
- ❖ have limited exposure to sunlight or insufficient vitamin D in their diet.
- ❖ do not get enough physical activity.
- ❖ have a family history of osteoporosis.
- ❖ are thin and small-boned.
- ❖ are white or of Eurasian ancestry.
- ❖ smoke.
- ❖ consume caffeine (consistently more than three cups a day of coffee, tea, cola).

❖ drink alcoholic beverages (consistently more than two drinks a day).
❖ take excess amounts of certain medications (cortisone and prednisone, anti-convulsants, thyroid hormone, antacids containing aluminum).

If you are at risk for osteoporosis, your doctor may send you for a bone density test, an X-ray scan of the spine and hips that measures density by the amount of light that passes through the bones. Your bone density is then compared with an average bone density to assess whether you are normal, above normal, or below normal for someone your age. The Canadian Task Force on Preventive Health Care is awaiting the results of the Canadian Multicentre Osteoporosis Study to be released in 2002 before passing judgment on the validity of the test.

PREVENTING OSTEOPOROSIS

❖ Make the appropriate lifestyle choices: live smoke-free, drink alcohol in moderation.
❖ Get enough calcium, which is necessary for strong bones.
❖ Include weight-bearing exercise – weight training, walking, aerobics, jogging – in your physical activities.
❖ If you are a post-menopausal woman, consider hormone replacement therapy.

TREATING OSTEOPOROSIS

For postmenopausal women, hormone replacement therapy is recommended as a treatment because it has been shown to actually increase bone density. A relatively new class of drugs –

bisphosphonates – is also proven to be an effective treatment. Two types, etidronate (Didrocal/Didronel) and alendronate (Fosamax), are approved in Canada. Bisphosphonates slow down the bone erosion process without affecting bone-building cells; consequently, your bone mass will increase.

Resources

GENERAL

Canadian AIDS Society
National Office
130 Albert Street, Suite 900
Ottawa, Ontario
KIP 5G4
(613) 230-3580
(613) 563-4998 (fax)
www.cnaids.ca

Canadian Medical Association
1867 Alta Vista Drive
Ottawa, Ontario
KIG 3Y6
(613) 731-9331
(613) 731-7314 (fax)
Toll Free: 1-800-663-7336
www.cma.ca

Canadian MedicAlert Foundation
National Office
250 Ferrand Street, 301
Toronto, Ontario
M3C 3G8
(416) 696-0267
(416) 696-9340 (fax)
Toll Free: 1-800-668-1507
www.medicalert.ca
E-mail: medinfo@medicalert.ca

Canadian Naturopathic Association
1255 Sheppard Avenue East
Toronto, Ontario
M2K IE2
(416) 496-8633
(416) 496-8634 (fax)
www.naturopathicassoc.ca

The College of Family Physicians of
Canada
2630 Skymark Avenue
Mississauga, Ontario
L4W 5A4
(905) 629-0900
(905) 629-0893 (fax)
www.cfpc.ca

IVF Canada (in vitro fertilization)
2347 Kennedy Road, Suite 304
Scarborough, Ontario
MIT 3T8
(416) 754-8742
www.ivfcanada.com
E-mail: info@ivfcanada.com

The Society of Obstetricians and
Gynaecologists of Canada (SOGC)
774 Echo Drive
Ottawa, Ontario
KIS 5N8
(613) 730-4192
(613) 730-4314 (fax)
www.sogc.medical.org/

*The Complete Canadian Health
Guide*
June Engel, PHD
Key Porter Books, Toronto, 1999

*Patient Power: The Smart Patient's
Guide to Health Care*
Patricia Parsons, BN, MSC, and Arthur
Parsons, MD
University of Toronto Press, Toronto,
1997

ADDICTIONS/SUBSTANCE ABUSE

Alcoholics Anonymous (AA)
National Office
234 Eglinton Avenue East, Suite 202
Toronto, Ontario
M4P 1K5
(416) 487-5591
(416) 487-5855 (fax)
www.alcoholics-anonymous.org

Canadian Centre on Substance Abuse
75 Albert Street, Suite 300
Ottawa, Ontario
K1P 5E7
(613) 235-4048
(613) 235-8101 (fax)
www.ccsa.ca

Centre for Addiction and Mental
  Health
33 Russell Street
Toronto, Ontario
M5S 2S1
(416) 595-6385
(416) 595-6881 (fax)
www.camh.net

National Eating Disorder Information
  Centre
Canada Building, 344 Slater Street,
  10th Floor
Ottawa, Ontario
K1R 7Y3
(613) 995-2298
(613) 995-2097 (fax)
www.nfpc-cnpa.gc.ca

Tobacco Facts
www.tobaccofacts.org

AGING

Canadian Dental Association
1815 Alta Vista Drive
Ottawa, Ontario
K1G 3Y6
(613) 523-1770
(613) 523-7736 (fax)
Toll Free: 1-800-267-6354
www.ceda-adc.ca

Canadian Dermatology Association
774 Promenade Echo Drive
Ottawa, Ontario
K1S 5N8
(514) 931-3617
(514) 933-8798 (fax)
www.derm.ubc.ca/jcms

Canadian Ophthamological Society
1525 Carling Avenue, Suite 610
Ottawa, Ontario
K1Z 8R9
(613) 729-6779
(613) 729-7209 (fax)
Toll Free: 1-800-267-5763
www.eyesight.ca

ALZHEIMER'S DISEASE

Alzheimer's Society
National Office
20 Eglinton West, Suite 1200
Toronto, Ontario
M4R 1K8
(416) 488-8772
(416) 488-3778 (fax)
Toll Free: 1-800-616-8816
www.alzheimer.ca
E-mail: info@alzheimer.ca

ANDROPAUSE

Andropause Information Request Line
1-877-550-3931

Canadian Andropause Society
Laval Research Centre
2705 Laurier Boulevard, Room T3-67
Ste-Foy, Quebec
G1V 4G2
(418) 656-4141 EXT. 6241
(418) 654-2215 (fax)

Canadian Urological Association
Health Sciences Centre, Room GE446
820 Sherbrook Street
Winnipeg, Manitoba
R3A 1R7
(204) 787-3677

*Male Menopause: Restoring Vitality
and Virility*
Malcolm Curruthers, MD
HarperCollins Publishers, London,
1996

Understanding Men's Passages
Gail Sheehy
Random House, New York, 1998

ARTHRITIS

The Arthritis Society
National Office
393 University Avenue, Suite 1700
Toronto, Ontario
M5G 1E6
(416) 979-7228
(416) 979-8366 (fax)
Toll Free: 1-800-321-1433
www.arthritis.ca
E-mail: info@arthritis.ca

ASTHMA/ALLERGIES

Allergy-Asthma Information
  Association
130 Bridgeland Avenue, Suite 424
Toronto, Ontario
M6A 1Z4
(416) 783-8944
(416) 783-7538 (fax)
Toll Free: 1-800-611-7011
www.cadvision.com/allergy

The Asthma Society of Canada
130 Bridgeland Avenue, Suite 425
Toronto, Ontario
M6A 1Z4
(416) 787-4050
(416) 787-5807 (fax)
Asthma InfoLine: 1-800-787-3880
www.asthmasociety.com/

Canadian Lung Association
1900 City Park Drive
Gloucester, Ontario
K1J 1A3
(613) 747-6776
(613) 747-7430 (fax)
www.lung.ca
E-mail: info@lung.ca

Toll Free Lung Health Information
  Line
1-800-972-2636

CANCER

Breast Implant Line of Canada
56 Touraine Avenue
Toronto, Ontario
M3H 1R2
(416) 636-6618

Canadian Breast Cancer Foundation
790 Bay Street, Suite 100
Toronto, Ontario
M4P 2H0
(416) 596-6773
(416) 596-7857 (fax)
Toll Free: 1-800-387-9816
www.cbcf.org

Canadian Cancer Society
National Office
10 Alcorn Avenue, Suite 200
Toronto, Ontario
M4V 3B1
(416) 961-7223
(416) 961-4189 (fax)
www.cancer.ca

Cancer Information Service
1-888-939-3333 (24 hour)

Health Canada's Cancer Bureau
www.hcsc.gc.ca/hpb/lcdc/c/index.html

National Ovarian Cancer Association
620 University Avenue
Toronto, Ontario
M5G 2L7
(416) 971-9800
(416) 971-6888 (fax)

Oncolink
www.oncolink.upenn.edu

COSMETIC SURGERY

Canadian Society for Aesthetic
   (Cosmetic) Plastic Surgery
4650 Highway #7
Woodbridge, Ontario
L4L 1S7
(905) 831-7750
(905) 831-7248 (fax)
Toll Free: 1-800-263-4429

Canadian Society of Plastic Surgeons
30 St. Joseph Boulevard East, Suite 520
Montreal, Quebec
H2T 1G9
(514) 843-5415
(514) 843-7005 (fax)
Toll Free: 1-800-665-5415

DIABETES

Canadian Diabetes Association
National Office
15 Toronto Street, Suite 800
Toronto, Ontario
M5C 2E3
(416) 363-3373
(416) 214-1899 (fax)
Toll Free 1-800-BANTING
www.diabetes.ca
E-mail: info@cda-nat.org

*Managing Your Diabetes: The Only
   Guide to Type II Diabetes for
   Canadians*
Sara M. Rosenthal
Macmillan Canada, Toronto, 1998

EAT TO BEAT DISEASE

Canadian Cancer Society
National Office
10 Alcorn Avenue, Suite 200
Toronto, Ontario
M4V 3B1
(416) 961-7223
(416) 961-4189 (fax)
www.cancer.ca

Canadian Diabetes Association
National Office
15 Toronto Street, Suite 800
Toronto, Ontario
M5C 2E3
(416) 363-3373
(416) 214-1899 (fax)
Toll Free: 1-800-BANTING
www.diabetes.ca
E-mail: info@cda-nat.org

The Canadian Health Food
    Association
550 Alden Road, Suite 205
Markham, Ontario
L3R 6A8
(905) 479-6939
(905) 479-1516 (fax)
Toll Free: 1-800-661-4510
www.chfa.ca

Heart and Stroke Foundation
    of Canada
222 Queen Street, Suite 1402
Ottawa, Ontario
K1P 5V9
(613) 569-4361
(613) 569-3278 (fax)
Toll Free: 1-888-HSF-INFO
www.hsf.ca

Osteoporosis Society of Canada
33 Laird Drive
Toronto, Ontario
M4G 3S9
(416) 696-2817
Toll Free: 1-800-463-6842
www.osteoporosis.ca

ENDOMETRIOSIS

Endometriosis Association
8585 North 76th Place
Milwaukee, Wisconsin
53223
(414) 355-2200
(414) 355-6065 (fax)
Toll Free: 1-800-922-3636
www.endometriosisassn.org

Endometriosis.org
www.endometriosis.org

Infertility Awareness Association of
    Canada
1 Nicholas Street, Suite 406
Ottawa, Ontario
K1N 7B7
(613) 244-7222
(613) 244-8908 (fax)
Toll Free: 1-800-263-2929
www.fox.nstn.ca/~iaac
E-mail: iaac@fox.nstn.ca

The Society of Obstetricians and
    Gynaecologists of Canada (SOGC)
774 Echo Drive
Ottawa, Ontario
K1S 5N8
(613) 730-4192
(613) 730-4314 (fax)
sogc.medical.org

EXERCISE

Canada's Physical Activity Guide to
    Healthy Active Living
1-888-334-9769 (to order)
www.paguide.com

Canadian Society for Exercise
   Physiology
185 Somerset Street, Suite 202
Ottawa, Ontario
K2P 0J2
(613) 234-3755
(613) 234-3565 (fax)
Toll Free: 1-877-651-3755
htpp://www.csep.ca

The Canadian Volkssport Federation
P.O. Box 2668, Station D
Ottawa, Ontario
KIP 5W7
(902) 466-4421
(902) 434-4221 (fax)
www.chebucto.ns.ca/Recreation/CVF

ParticipAction
40 Dundas Street West, Suite 220
Toronto, Ontario
M5G 2C2
(416) 954-1212
(416) 954-4949 (fax)

EYE CARE

Canadian Ophthamological Society
1525 Carling Avenue, Suite 610
Ottawa, Ontario
KIZ 8R9
(613) 729-6779
(613) 729-7209 (fax)
Toll Free: 1-800-267-5763
www.eyesight.ca

HEARING

The Canadian Hearing Society
271 Spadina Road
Toronto, Ontario
M5R 2V3
(416) 964-9595
(416) 964-0023 (TDD)
(416) 928-2506 (fax)
www.chs.ca
E-mail: info@chs.ca

HEART HEALTH

Heart and Stroke Foundation
   of Canada
222 Queen Street, Suite 1402
Ottawa, Ontario
KIP 5V9
(613) 569-4361
(613) 569-3278 (fax)
Toll Free: 1-888-HSF-INFO
www.hsf.ca

*Bonnie Stern's Simply HeartSmart
   Cooking*
Bonnie Stern
Random House Canada, Toronto,
   1994

*The Canadian Family Guide to
   Stroke Prevention, Treatment and
   Recovery*
(Adapted for Canadians by The Heart
   and Stroke Foundation of Canada)
Random House of Canada, Toronto,
   1996

*The HeartSmart Shopper: Nutrition
   on the Run*
Ramona Josephson
Douglas & McIntyre, Vancouver, 1997

HEPATITIS C

Canadian Liver Foundation
National Office
365 Bloor Street East, Suite 200
Toronto, Ontario
M4W 3L4
(416) 964-1953
(416) 964-0024 (fax)
Toll Free: 1-800-563-5483
www.liver.ca
E-mail: clf@liver.ca

HORMONE REPLACEMENT THERAPY (HRT)

Canadian Women's Health Network
419 Graham Avenue, Suite 203
Winnipeg, Manitoba
R3C 0M3
(204) 942-5500
(204) 989-2355 (fax)
Clearinghouse: 1-888-818-9172
www.cwhn.ca

North American Menopause Society
P.O. Box 94527
Cleveland, Ohio
44101-4527
(216) 844-8748
(216) 844-8708 (fax)
Toll Free: 1-800-774-5342
www.menopause.org
E-mail: info@menopause.org

The Society of Obstetricians and
   Gynaecologists of Canada (SOGC)
774 Echo Drive
Ottawa, Ontario
KIS 5N8
(613) 730-4192
(613) 730-4314 (fax)
sogc.medical.org

NUTRITION

Dietitians of Canada
480 University Avenue
Toronto, Ontario
M5F IV2
(416) 596-0857
(416) 596-0603 (fax)

Health Canada - Nutrition
www.hc-sc.gc.ca/hppb.nutrition

National Eating Disorder Information
   Centre
Canada Building, 344 Slater Street,
   10th Floor
Ottawa, Ontario
KIR 7Y3
(613) 995-2298
(613) 995-2097 (fax)
www.nfpc-cnpa.gc.ca

National Institute of Nutrition
265 Carling Avenue, Suite 302
Ottawa, Ontario
KIS 2EI
(613) 235-3355
(613) 235-7032 (fax)
www.nin.ca

Anne Lindsay's New Light Cooking
Anne Lindsay in cooperation with
   Denise Beatty, RD, and the
   Canadian Medical Association
Ballantine Books, Toronto, 1998

*Becoming Vegetarian: The Complete
   Guide to Adopting a Healthy
   Vegetarian Diet*
Vestano Melina, RD, Brenda Davis, RD,
   and Victoria Harrison, RD
Macmillan Canada, Toronto, 1994

*Canadian Living's Best: 30 Minutes
  and Light*
Elizabeth Baird and the Test Kitchen
  Staff of *Canadian Living* magazine
Ballantine Books, Toronto, 1998

*Canadian Living's Best: Vegetarian
  Dishes*
Elizabeth Baird and the Test Kitchen
  Staff of *Canadian Living* magazine
Ballantine Books, Toronto, 1998

The Enlightened Eater
Rosie Schwartz
Macmillan Canada, Toronto, 1994

OSTEOPOROSIS

Osteoporosis Society of Canada
33 Laird Drive
Toronto, Ontario
M4G 3S9
(416) 696-2817
Toll Free: 1-800-463-6842
www.osteoporosis.ca

PAIN

Canadian Chiropractic Association
1396 Eglinton Avenue West
Toronto, Ontario
M6C 2E4
(416) 781-5656
(416) 781-7344 (fax)
Toll Free: 1-800-668-2076
www.ccachiro.org

Canadian Massage Therapist Alliance
365 Bloor Street East, Suite 1807
Toronto, Ontario
M4W 3L4
(416) 968-2149
(416) 968-6818 (fax)

The Migraine Association of Canada
365 Bloor Street East, Suite 1912
Toronto, Ontario
M4W 3L4
(416) 920-4916
(416) 920-3677 (fax)
Toll Free: 1-800-663-3557
www.migraine.ca/

North American Chronic Pain
  Association of Canada
150 Central Park Drive, Unit 105
Brampton, Ontario
L6T 2T9
(905) 846-0958
(905) 793-8781 (fax)
www3.sympatico.ca/nacpac

University Carpal Syndrome Centre
700 University Avenue, Shopping
  Concourse
Toronto, Ontario
M5G 1Z5
(416) 596-1773
(416) 398-7957 (fax)

PERIMENOPAUSE &
MENOPAUSE

North American Menopause Society
P.O. Box 94527
Cleveland, Ohio
44101-4527
(216) 844-8748
(216) 844-8708 (fax)
Toll Free: 1-800-774-5342
www.menopause.org
E-mail: info@menopause.org

Osteoporosis Society of Canada
33 Laird Drive
Toronto, Ontario
M4G 3S9
(416) 696-2817
Toll Free: 1-800-463-6842
www.osteoporosis.ca

The Society of Obstetricians and
 Gynaecologists of Canada (SOGC)
774 Echo Drive
Ottawa, Ontario
K1S 5N8
(613) 730-4192
(613) 730-4314 (fax)
sogc.medical.org

Could it Be . . . Perimenopause?
Dr. Steven R. Goldstein and Laurie
 Ashner
Little, Brown and Company, Boston,
 1998

*Menopause: A Naturopathic
 Approach to the Transitional Years*
Karen Jensen, MD, ND
Prentice Hall Canada, Scarborough,
 1999

*Menopause: The Complete Practical
 Guide to Managing Your Life
 and Maintaining Physical and
 Emotional Well-Being*
Miriam Stoppard, MD
Random House Canada, Toronto,
 1994

*Perimenopause: Changes in Women's
 Health After 35*
James E. Huston, MD, and Darlene L.
 Lanka, MD
New Harbinger Press, California,
 1997

Understanding Menopause
Janine O'Leary Cobb
Key Porter Books, Toronto, 1996

PROSTATE HEALTH

Canadian Cancer Society
National Office
10 Alcorn Avenue, Suite 200
Toronto, Ontario
M4V 3B1
(416) 961-7223
(416) 961-4189 (fax)
www.cancer.ca

Canadian Urological Association
Health Sciences Centre
Room GE446
820 Sherbrook Street
Winnipeg, Manitoba
R3A 1R7
(204) 787-3677
(204) 787-3040 (fax)

*Midlife Man: A Not-so-threatening
 Guide to Health and Sex for Man
 at His Peak*
Art Hister, MD
Graystone Books, Vancouver, 1998

*Private Parts: An Owner's Guide to
 the Male Anatomy*
Yosh Taguchi, MD
McClelland & Stewart, Toronto, 1996

SEXUAL/REPRODUCTIVE HEALTH

Canadian Fertility and Andrology
 Society
2065 Alexandre de Sève, Suite 409
Montreal, Quebec
H2L 2W5
(514) 524-9009
www.cfas.ca

Infertility Awareness Association
   of Canada
1 Nicholas Street, Suite 406
Ottawa, Ontario
KIN 7B7
(416) 244-7222
Toll Free: 1-800-263-2929
www.fox.nstn.ca/~iaac
E-mail: iaac@fox.nstn.ca

Planned Parenthood Association
   of Canada
National Office
1 Nicholas Street, Suite 430
Ottawa, Ontario
KIN 7B7
(613) 241-4474
(613) 241-7550 (fax)
www.ppfc.ca

SIECCAN (The Sex Information and
   Education Council of Canada)
850 Coxwell Avenue
Toronto, Ontario
M4R 5R1
(416) 466-5304
(416) 778-0785 (fax)

SKIN CARE

Canadian Dermatology Association
774 Promenade Echo Drive
Ottawa, Ontario
KIS 5N8
(514) 931-3617
(514) 933-8798 (fax)
www.derm.ubc.ca/jcms

The Life of the Skin: What It Hides,
   What It Reveals and How It
   Communicates
Arthur K. Balin & Loretta Pratt Balin
Bantam Books, 1997

SLEEP

Canadian Sleep Society
National Office
3080 Yonge Street, Suite 5055
Toronto, Ontario
M4N 3N1
(416) 483-6260
(416) 483-7081 (fax)

Sleep/Wake Disorders Canada
National Office
3080 Yonge Street, Suite 5055
Toronto, Ontario
M4N 3N1
(416) 483-9451
(416) 483-7081 (fax)
www.geocities.com/~sleepwake

STRESS/DEPRESSION

Canadian Institute of Stress
Box 665, Station U
Toronto, Ontario
M8Z 5Y9
(416) 236-4218
(416) 237-1828 (fax)

Canadian Mental Health Association
National Office
2160 Yonge Street, 3rd Floor
Toronto, Ontario
M4S 2Z3
(416) 484-7750
(416) 484-4617 (fax)
www.cmha.ca

Index